Lead Like Carnegie

Timeless *Leadership Principles* for the *Contemporary Leader*

Dale Carnegie

Published by
Rupa Publications India Pvt. Ltd 2024
7/16, Ansari Road, Daryaganj
New Delhi 110002

Sales centres:
Bengaluru Chennai
Hyderabad Jaipur Kathmandu
Kolkata Mumbai Prayagraj

Edition copyright © Rupa Publications India Pvt. Ltd 2024

All rights reserved.
No part of this publication may be reproduced, transmitted,
or stored in a retrieval system, in any form or by any means,
electronic, mechanical, photocopying, recording or otherwise, without
the prior permission of the publisher.

P-ISBN: 978-93-5702-904-9
E-ISBN: 978-93-5702-692-5

Second impression 2024

10 9 8 7 6 5 4 3 2

Printed in India

This book is sold subject to the condition that it shall not, by way of
trade or otherwise, be lent, resold, hired out, or otherwise circulated,
without the publisher's prior consent, in any form of binding or
cover other than that in which it is published.

Contents

1. Finding the Leader in You — 7
2. If You Don't Do This, You Are Headed for Trouble — 18
3. Acquiring Confidence Before an Audience — 28
4. Fluency through Preparation — 35
5. Earning the Right to Talk — 40
6. Vitalizing the Talk — 56
7. Influencing the Crowd — 66
8. The Voice — 73
9. The Sin of Monotony — 82
10. Making It Happen — 86
11. Feeling and Enthusiasm — 89
12. A Sure Way of Making Enemies—and How to Avoid It — 98
13. Handling Mistakes, Complaints and Criticism — 109
14. The Movies Do It. TV Does It. Why Don't You Do It? — 121
15. Making People Glad While Doing What You Want — 126
16. Give a Dog a Good Name — 132
17. Riding the Winged Horse — 137
18. Teaming up for Tomorrow — 147
19. If You Must Find Fault, This Is the Way to Begin — 161
20. Find Yourself and Be Yourself — 168

1

FINDING THE LEADER IN YOU

Fred Wilpon is the president of the New York Mets baseball team. One afternoon, Wilpon was leading a group of school children on a tour of Shea Stadium. He let them stand behind home plate. He took them into the team dugouts. He walked them through the private passage to the clubhouse. As the final stop on his tour, Wilpon wanted to take the students into the stadium bull pen, where the pitchers warm up.

But right outside the bull pen gate, the group was stopped by a uniformed security guard.

'The bull pen isn't open to the public,' the guard told Wilpon, obviously unaware of who he was. 'I'm sorry, but you can't go out there.'

Now, Fred Wilpon certainly had the power to get what he wanted right then and there. He could have berated the poor security guard for failing to recognize such an important person as himself. With a dramatic flourish, Wilpon could have whipped out his top-level security pass and shown the wide-eyed children how much weight he carried at Shea.

Wilpon did none of that. He led the students to the far side of the stadium and took them into the bull pen through another gate.

Why did he bother to do that? Wilpon didn't want to

embarrass the security guard. The man, after all, was doing his job and doing it well. Later that afternoon, Wilpon even sent off a handwritten note, thanking the guard for showing such concern.

Had Wilpon chosen instead to yell or cause a scene, the guard might well have ended up feeling resentful, and no doubt his work would have suffered as a result. Wilpon's gentle approach made infinitely more sense. The guard felt great about the compliment. And you can bet he'll recognize Wilpon the next time the two of them happen to meet.

Fred Wilpon is a leader and not just because of the title he holds or the salary he earns. What makes him a leader of men and women is how he has learned to interact.

IMPORTANCE OF BEING A PEOPLE PERSON

In the past, people in the business world didn't give much thought to the true meaning of leadership. The boss was the boss, and he was in charge. Period. End of discussion.

Well-run companies—no one ever spoke about 'well-led companies'—were the ones that operated in an almost militaristic style. Orders were delivered from above and passed down through the ranks.

Remember Mr. Dithers from the *Blondie* comic strip? *'BUM-STEAD!'* he would scream, and young Dagwood would come rushing into the boss's office like a frightened puppy. Lots of real-life companies operated that way for years. The companies that weren't run like army platoons were barely run at all. They just puttered along as they always had, secure in some little niche of a market that hadn't been challenged for years. The message from above was always, 'If it ain't broke, why fix it?'

The people responsible sat in their offices and managed what they could. That's what they were expected to do—to 'manage'. Maybe they steered the organizations a few degrees to the left or a few degrees to the right. Usually they tried to deal with whatever obvious problems presented themselves, and then called it a day.

Back when the world was a simpler place, management like this was fine. Rarely visionary, but fine, as life rolled predictably along.

But mere management simply isn't enough anymore. The world is too unpredictable, too volatile, too fast-moving for such an uninspired approach. What's needed now is something much deeper than old-fashioned business management. What's needed is *leadership, to help people achieve what they are capable of, to establish a vision for the future, to encourage, to coach and to mentor, and to establish and maintain successful relationships.*

'Back when businesses operated in a more stable environment, management skills were sufficient,' says Harvard Business School professor John Quelch. 'But when the business environment becomes volatile, when the waters are uncharted, when your mission requires greater flexibility than you ever imagined it would—that's when leadership skills become critical.'

'The change is already taking place, and I'm not sure all organizations are ready for it,' says Bill Makahilahila, Director of Human Resources at SGS-Thomson Microelectronics, Inc., a leading semiconductor manufacturer. 'The position called "manager" may not exist too much longer, and the concept of "leadership" will be redefined. Companies today are going through that struggle. They are realizing, as they begin to downsize their operations and reach for greater productivity, that facilitative skills are going to be primary. Good communication, interpersonal skills, the ability to coach, model, and build teams—all of that requires more and better leaders.

'You can't do it by directive anymore. It has to be by influence. It takes real "people skills."'

BALANCE YOUR WORK LIFE AND SOCIAL LIFE

Many people still have a narrow understanding of what leadership really is. You say, 'leader' and they think *general, president, prime minister, or chairman of the board.* Obviously, people in those exalted positions are expected to lead, an expectation they meet with varying levels of success. But the fact of the matter is that leadership does not begin and end at the very top. It is every bit as important, perhaps more important, in the places most of us live and work.

Organizing a small work team, energizing an office support staff, keeping things happy at home—those are the front lines of leadership. Leadership is never easy. But thankfully, something else is also true: every one of us has the potential to be a leader every day.

The team facilitator, the middle manager, the account executive, the customer-service operator, the person who works in the mail room—just about anyone who ever comes in contact with others has good reason to learn how to lead.

To an enormous degree their leadership skills will determine how much success they achieve and how happy they will be. Not just at work, either. Families, charity groups, sports teams, civic associations, social clubs, you name it—every one of those organizations has a tremendous need for dynamic leadership.

Steve Jobs and Steve Wozniak were a couple of blue-jeans-wearing kids from California, ages twenty-one and twenty-six. They weren't rich, they had absolutely no business training, and they were hoping to get started in an industry that barely existed at the time.

The year was 1976, before most people ever thought about buying computers for their homes. In those days the entire home-computer business added up to just a few brainy hobbyists, the original 'computer nerds'. So when Jobs and Wozniak scraped together thirteen hundred dollars by selling a van and two calculators and opened Apple Computer, Inc., in Job's garage, the odds against their smashing success seemed awfully long.

But these two young entrepreneurs had a vision, a clear idea of what they believed they could achieve. 'Computers aren't just for nerds anymore,' they announced. 'Computers are going to be the bicycle of the mind. Low-cost computers are for everyone.'

From day one the Apple founders kept their vision intact, and they communicated it at every turn. They hired people who understood the vision and let them share in its rewards. They lived and breathed and talked the vision. Even when the company got stalled—when the retailers said no thank you, when the manufacturing people said no way, when the bankers said no more—Apple's visionary leaders never backed down.

Eventually the world came around. Six years after Apple's founding, the company was selling 650,000 personal computers a year. Wozniak and Jobs were dynamic personal leaders, years ahead of their time.

It's not just new organizations, however, that need visionary leadership. In the early 1980s, Corning, Incorporated, was caught in a terrible squeeze. The Corning name still meant something in kitchenware, but that name was being seriously undermined. The company's manufacturing technology was outmoded. Its market share was down. Corning customers were defecting by the thousands to foreign firms. And the company's stodgy management didn't seem to have a clue.

That's when Chairman James R. Houghton concluded that Corning needed a whole new vision, and he proposed one. Houghton recalls, 'We had an outside consultant who was working with me and my new team as our resident shrink. He was really a facilitator, a wonderful guy who kept hammering on the quality issue as something we had to get into.

'We were in one of those terrible group meetings and everybody was very depressed. I got up and announced that we were going to spend about ten million bucks that we didn't have. We were going to set up our own quality institute. We were going to get going on this.

'There were a lot of different things that put me over the top. But I am fast to admit, I just had a gut feeling that it was right. I had no idea of the implications, none, and how important they would be.'

Houghton knew that Corning had to improve the quality of its manufacturing and had to speed up their delivery time. What the chairman did was take a risk. He sought advice from the best experts in the world—his own employees. Not just the manager and the company engineers. Houghton brought in the line employees too. He put a representative team together and told them to redesign Corning's entire manufacturing process—if that's what it took to bring the company around.

The answer, the team decided after six months of work, was to redesign certain plants to reduce defects on the assembly line and make the machines faster to retool. The teams also reorganized the way Corning kept its inventories to get a faster turnaround. The results were astounding. When Houghton launched these changes, irregularities in a new fiber-optics coating process were running eight hundred parts per million.

Four years later that measure fell to zero. In two more years delivery time was cut from weeks to days, and in the space of four years Corning's return on equity nearly doubled. Houghton's vision had literally turned the company around.

Business theorists Warren Bennis and Burt Nanus have studied hundreds of successful organizations, large and small, focussing on the way in which they are led. 'A leader,' the two men write, 'must first have developed a mental image of a possible and desirable future state of the organization. This image, which we call a vision, may be as vague as a dream or as precise as a goal or a mission statement.' The critical point, Bennis and Nanus explain, 'is that a vision articulates a view of a realistic, credible, attractive future for the organization, a condition that is better in some important ways than what now exists.'

SINCERITY MAKES A DIFFERENCE

Leaders ask: Where is this work team heading? What does this division stand for? Who are we trying to serve? How can we improve the quality of our work? The specific answers will be as different as the people being led, as different as the leaders themselves. What's most important is that the questions are asked.

There is no one correct way to lead, and talented leaders come in many personality types. They are loud or quiet, funny or severe, tough or gentle, boisterous or shy. They come from all ages, any race, both sexes, and every kind of group there is.

The idea isn't just to identify the most successful leader you can find and then slavishly model yourself after him or her. That strategy is doomed from the start. You are unlikely ever to rise above a poor imitation of the person you are pretending to be.

The leadership techniques that will work best for you are the ones you nurture inside.

Fred Ebb is a Tony Award-winning composer whose hit Broadway shows include *Cabaret*, *Kiss of the Spider Woman*, *Chicago* and *Zorba*. Frequently, young songwriters come to Ebb for professional guidance. 'I always tell them to follow the advice that Irving Berlin had for George Gershwin,' Ebb says.

It seems that when Berlin and Gershwin first met, Berlin was already famous and Gershwin was just a struggling young composer working on Tin Pan Alley for thirty-five dollars a week. Impressed by Gershwin's obvious talent, Berlin offered the young man a job as his musical secretary at almost triple what Gershwin was earning writing songs.

'But don't take the job,' Berlin advised. 'If you do, you may develop into a second-rate Berlin. But if you insist on being yourself, someday you will become a first-rate Gershwin.'

Gershwin stuck with Gershwin, of course, and American popular music reached new heights. 'Don't try to imitate others,' Ebb tells his protégés. 'Never stop being yourself.'

Often what this requires is figuring out who you really are and putting that insight thoughtfully to work. This is so important it's worth a bit of quiet reflection. Ask yourself the question in a straightforward way: what personal qualities do I possess that can be turned into the qualities of leadership?

For Robert L. Crandall, one of those qualities is a keen ability to anticipate change. Crandall, the chairman of AMR Corporation, piloted American Airlines through an extremely turbulent era in the air-travel business.

Olympic gymnast Mary Lou Retton got a big boost from her natural enthusiasm. She leapt out of a small town in West Virginia and landed in the hearts of people everywhere.

In the case of Hugh Downs, the veteran ABC newsman,

one of these leadership qualities was his down-to-earth humility. Downs managed to build a huge career for himself in the highly competitive business of broadcasting and still remain a gentleman.

Whatever those qualities are for you—a dogged persistence, a steel-trap mind, a great imagination, a positive attitude, a strong sense of values—let them blossom into leadership. And remember that actions are far more powerful than words.

Arthur Ashe was a world-class tennis player and a world-class father—a true leader in those and other realms. He too believed in leading by example.

'My wife and I talk about this with our six-year-old daughter,' Ashe said in an interview just before his death. 'Children are much more impressed by what they see you do than by what you say,' he said. 'Children at that age certainly keep you honest. If you have been preaching one thing all along and all of a sudden you don't do it, they're going to bring it right up in your face.

'I tell her it's not polite to eat with your elbows on the table. Then after dinner I'm putting my elbows up. She says, "Daddy, your elbows are on the table." You have to be man enough, or woman enough, to say, "You're right," and take your elbows down. In fact, that's an even stronger learning experience than her hearing it. It means that she did listen in the past. She understands it. And she recognizes it when she sees it. But it takes actions, rather than mere words, to accomplish that.'

A leader establishes standards and then sticks to them. Douglas A. Warner III, for instance, has always insisted on what he calls 'full transparency'.

'When you come in to make a proposal to me,' says Warner, president of J.P. Morgan & Co., 'assume that everything that you just told me appears tomorrow on the front page of the

Wall Street Journal. Are you going to be proud to have handled this transaction or handled this situation in the way you just recommended, assuming full transparency? If the answer to that is no, then we're going to stop right here and examine what the problem is.' That is a mark of leadership.

Well-focussed, self-confident leadership like that is what turns a vision into reality. Just ask Mother Teresa. She was a young Catholic nun, teaching high school in an upper-middle-class section of Calcutta. But she kept looking out the window and seeing the lepers on the street. 'I saw fear in their eyes,' she said. 'The fear they would never be loved, the fear they would never get adequate medical attention.'

She could not shake that fear out of her mind. She knew she had to leave the security of the convent, go out into the streets, and set up homes of peace for the lepers of India. Over the years to come, Mother Teresa and her Missionaries of Charity have cared for 149,000 people with leprosy, dispensing medical attention and unconditional love.

One December day, after addressing the United Nations, Mother Teresa went to visit a maximum-security prison in upstate New York. While inside she spoke with four inmates who had AIDS. She knew at once that these were the lepers of today.

She got back to New York City on the Monday before Christmas, and she went straight to City Hall to see Mayor Edward Koch. She asked the mayor if he would telephone the governor, Mario Cuomo. 'Governor,' she said, after Koch handed her the phone, 'I'm just back from Sing Sing, and four prisoners there have AIDS. I'd like to open up an AIDS center. Would you mind releasing those four prisoners to me? I'd like them to be the first four in the AIDS centre.'

'Well, Mother,' Cuomo said, 'we have forty-three cases of AIDS in the state prison system. I'll release all forty-three to you.'

'Okay,' she said. 'I'd like to start with just the four. Now let me tell you about the building I have in mind. Would you like to pay for it?'

'Okay,' Cuomo agreed, bowled over by this woman's intensity.

Then Mother Teresa turned to Mayor Koch, and she said to him, 'Today is Monday. I'd like to open this on Wednesday. We're going to need some permits cleared. Could you please arrange those?'

Koch just looked at this tiny woman standing in his office and shook his head back and forth. 'As long as you don't make me wash the floors,' the mayor said.

THE FIRST STEP TOWARDS SUCCESS IS IDENTIFYING YOUR OWN LEADERSHIP STRENGTHS.

POINTS TO REMEMBER

1. Redefining the term 'leadership'.
2. Value of people skills in a leader.
3. Answers don't matter as much as questions do.

2

IF YOU DON'T DO THIS, YOU ARE HEADED FOR TROUBLE

Back in 1898, a tragic thing happened in Rockland County, New York. A child had died, and on this particular day the neighbours were preparing to go to the funeral. Jim Farley went out to the barn to hitch up his horse. The ground was covered with snow, the air was cold and snappy; the horse hadn't been exercised for days, and as he was led out to the watering trough, he wheeled playfully, kicked both his heels high in the air, and killed Jim Farley. So the little village of Stony Point had two funerals that week instead of one.

Jim Farley left behind him a widow and three boys, and a few hundred dollars in insurance.

His oldest boy, Jim, was ten, and he went to work in a brickyard, wheeling sand and pouring it into the moulds and turning the brick on edge to be dried by the sun. This boy Jim never had a chance to get much education. But with his natural geniality, he had a flair for making people like him, so he went into politics, and as the years went by, he developed an uncanny ability for remembering people's names.

He never saw the inside of a high school; but before he was 46 years of age, four colleges had honoured him with degrees and he had become chairman of the Democratic National Committee and Postmaster General of the United States.

I once interviewed Jim Farley and asked him the secret of his success. He said, 'Hard work,' and I said, 'Don't be funny.'

He then asked me what I thought was the reason for his success. I replied: 'I understand you can call ten thousand people by their first names.'

'No. You are wrong,' he said. 'I can call fifty thousand people by their first names.'

Make no mistake about it. That ability helped Mr Farley put Franklin D. Roosevelt in the White House when he managed Roosevelt's campaign in 1932.

During the years that Jim Farley travelled as a salesman for a gypsum concern, and during the years that he held office as town clerk in Stony Point, he built up a system for remembering names.

In the beginning, it was a very simple one. Whenever he met a new acquaintance, he found out his or her complete name and some facts about his or her family, business and political opinions. He fixed all these facts well in mind as part of the picture, and the next time he met that person, even if it was a year later, he was able to shake hands, inquire after the family and ask about the hollyhocks in the backyard. No wonder he developed a following!

For months before Roosevelt's campaign for President began, Jim Farley wrote hundreds of letters a day to people all over the western and northwestern states. Then he hopped onto a train and in 19 days covered 20 states and 12,000 miles, travelling by buggy, train, automobile and boat. He would drop into town to meet his people at lunch or breakfast, tea or dinner, and give them a 'heart-to-heart talk'. Then he'd dash off again on another leg of his journey.

As soon as he arrived back East, he wrote to one person

in each town he had visited, asking for a list of all the guests to whom he had talked. The final list contained thousands and thousands of names: yet each person on that list was paid the subtle flattery of getting a personal letter from James Farley. These letters began 'Dear Bill' or 'Dear Jane,' and they were always signed 'Jim'.

Jim Farley discovered early in life that the average person is more interested in his or her own name than in all the other names on earth put together. Remember that name and call it easily, and you have paid a subtle and very effective compliment. But forget it or misspell it—and you have placed yourself at a sharp disadvantage. For example, I once organised a public-speaking course in Paris and sent form letters to all the American residents in the city. French typists with apparently little knowledge of English filled in the names and naturally they made blunders. One man, the manager of a large American bank in Paris, wrote me a scathing rebuke because his name had been misspelled.

Sometimes it is difficult to remember a name, particularly if it is hard to pronounce. Rather than even try to learn it, many people ignore it or call the person by an easy nickname. Sid Levy called on a customer for some time whose name was Nicodemus Papadoulos. Most people just called him 'Nick'. Levy told us: 'I made a special effort to say his name over several times to myself before I made my call. When I greeted him by his full name, 'Good afternoon, Mr Nicodemus Papadoulos,' he was shocked. For what seemed like several minutes there was no reply from him at all. Finally, he said with tears rolling down his cheeks, "Mr Levy, in all the fifteen years I have been in this country, nobody has ever made the effort to call me by my right name."'

What was the reason for Andrew Carnegie's success?

DO YOUR HOMEWORK

He was called the Steel King; yet he himself knew little about the manufacture of steel. He had hundreds of people working for him who knew far more about steel than he did.

But he knew how to handle people, and that is what made him rich. Early in life, he showed a flair for organisation, a genius for leadership. By the time he was ten, he too had discovered the astounding importance people place on their own name. And he used that discovery to win cooperation. To illustrate: when he was a boy back in Scotland, he got hold of a rabbit, a mother rabbit. Presto! He soon had a whole nest of little rabbits—and nothing to feed them. But he had a brilliant idea. He told the boys and girls in the neighbourhood that if they would go out and pull enough clover and dandelions to feed the rabbits, he would name the bunnies in their honour.

The plan worked like magic, and Carnegie never forgot it.

Years later, he made millions by using the same psychology in business. For example, he wanted to sell steel rails to the Pennsylvania Railroad. J. Edgar Thomson was the president of the Pennsylvania Railroad then. So Andrew Carnegie built a huge steel mill in Pittsburgh and called it the 'Edgar Thomson Steel Works.'

Here is a riddle. See if you can guess it. When the Pennsylvania Railroad needed steel rails, where do you suppose J. Edgar Thomson bought them? From Sears, Roebuck? No. No. You're wrong. Guess again.

When Carnegie and George Pullman were battling each other for supremacy in the railroad sleeping-car business, the Steel King again remembered the lesson of the rabbits.

The Central Transportation Company, which Andrew Carnegie controlled, was fighting with the company that Pullman owned. Both were struggling to get the sleeping-car business of the Union Pacific Railroad, bucking each other, slashing prices and destroying all chance of profit. Both Carnegie and Pullman had gone to New York to see the board of directors of the Union Pacific. Meeting one evening in the St Nicholas Hotel, Carnegie said, 'Good evening, Mr Pullman, aren't we making a couple of fools of ourselves?'

'What do you mean?' Pullman demanded.

Then Carnegie expressed what he had on his mind—a merger of their two interests. He pictured in glowing terms the mutual advantages of working with, instead of against, each other. Pullman listened attentively, but he was not wholly convinced. Finally he asked, 'What would you call the new company?' and Carnegie replied promptly, 'Why, the Pullman Palace Car Company, of course.'

Pullman's face brightened. 'Come into my room,' he said. 'Let's talk it over.' That talk made industrial history.

This policy of remembering and honouring the names of his friends and business associates was one of the secrets of Andrew Carnegie's leadership. He was proud of the fact that he could call many of his factory workers by their first names, and he boasted that while he was personally in charge, no strike ever disturbed his flaming steel mills.

Benton Love, chairman of Texas Commerce Bancshares, believes that the bigger a corporation gets, the colder it becomes. 'One way to warm it up,' he said, 'is to remember people's names. The executive who tells me he can't remember names is at the same time telling me he can't remember a significant part of his business and is operating on quicksand.'

Karen Kirsch of Rancho Palos Verdes, California, a flight attendant for TWA, made it a practice to learn the names of as many passengers in her cabin as possible and use the name when serving them. This resulted in many compliments on her service expressed both to her directly and to the airline. One passenger wrote, 'I haven't flown TWA for some time, but I'm going to start flying nothing but TWA from now on. You make me feel that your airline has become a very personalized airline and that is important to me.'

People are so proud of their names that they strive to perpetuate them at any cost. Even blustering, hard-boiled old P.T. Barnum, the greatest showman of his time, disappointed because he had no sons to carry on his name, offered his grandson, C.H. Seeley, $25,000 dollars if he would call himself 'Barnum' Seeley.

For many centuries, nobles and magnates supported artists, musicians and authors so that their creative works would be dedicated to them.

Libraries and museums owe their richest collections to people who cannot bear to think that their names might perish from the memory of the race. The New York Public Library has its Astor and Lenox collections. The Metropolitan Museum perpetuates the names of Benjamin Altman and J.P. Morgan. And nearly every church is beautified by stained-glass windows commemorating the names of their donors. Many of the buildings on the campus of most universities bear the names of donors who contributed large sums of money for this honour.

Most people don't remember names, for the simple reason that they don't take the time and energy necessary to concentrate and repeat and fix names indelibly in their minds. They make excuses for themselves; they are too busy.

But they were probably no busier than Franklin D. Roosevelt, and he took time to remember and recall even the names of mechanics with whom he came into contact.

To illustrate: the Chrysler organization built a special car for Mr Roosevelt, who could not use a standard car because his legs were paralysed. W.F. Chamberlain and a mechanic delivered it to the White House. I have in front of me a letter from Mr Chamberlain relating his experiences. 'I taught President Roosevelt how to handle a car with a lot of unusual gadgets, but he taught me a lot about the fine art of handling people.

'When I called at the White House,' Mr Chamberlain writes, 'the President was extremely pleasant and cheerful. He called me by name, made me feel very comfortable, and particularly impressed me with the fact that he was vitally interested in things I had to show him and tell him. The car was so designed that it could be operated entirely by hand. A crowd gathered around to look at the car; and he remarked, "I think it is marvellous. All you have to do is to touch a button and it moves away and you can drive it without effort. I think it is grand—I don't know what makes it go. I'd love to have the time to tear it down and see how it works."

'When Roosevelt's friends and associates admired the machine, he said in their presence, "Mr Chamberlain, I certainly appreciate all the time and effort you have spent in developing this car. It is a mighty fine job." He admired the radiator, the special rear-vision mirror and clock, the special spotlight, the kind of upholstery, the sitting position of the driver's seat, the special suitcases in the trunk with his monogram on each suitcase. In other words, he took notice of every detail to which he knew I had given considerable thought. He made a point of bringing these various pieces of equipment to the attention of Mrs Roosevelt, Miss Perkins, the Secretary of Labour, and his secretary. He even brought the old White House porter into the picture by saying, "George, you want to take particularly good care of the suitcases."

'When the driving lesson was finished, the President turned

to me and said: "Well, Mr Chamberlain, I have been keeping the Federal Reserve Board waiting thirty minutes. I guess I had better get back to work."

'I took a mechanic with me to the White House. He was introduced to Roosevelt when he arrived. He didn't talk to the President, and Roosevelt heard his name only once. He was a shy chap, and he kept in the background. But before leaving us, the President looked for the mechanic, shook his hand, called him by name and thanked him for coming to Washington. And there was nothing perfunctory about his thanks. He meant what he said. I could feel that.

'A few days after returning to New York, I got an autographed photograph of President Roosevelt and a little note of thanks again expressing his appreciation for my assistance. How he found time to do it is a mystery to me.'

Franklin D. Roosevelt knew that one of the simplest, most obvious and most important ways of gaining goodwill was by remembering names and making people feel important—yet how many of us do it?

Half the time we are introduced to a stranger, we chat a few minutes and can't even remember his or her name by the time we say goodbye.

One of the first lessons a politician learns is this, 'To recall a voter's name is statesmanship. To forget it is oblivion.'

And the ability to remember names is almost as important in business and social contacts as it is in politics.

TRICK TO REMEMBER

Napoleon the Third, Emperor of France and nephew of the great Napoleon, boasted that in spite of all his royal duties he could remember the name of every person he met.

His technique? Simple. If he didn't hear the name distinctly, he said, 'So sorry. I didn't get the name clearly.' Then, if it was an unusual name, he would say, 'How is it spelled?'

During the conversation, he took the trouble to repeat the name several times, and tried to associate it in his mind with the person's features, expression and general appearance.

If the person was someone of importance, Napoleon went to even further pains. As soon as His Royal Highness was alone, he wrote the name down on a piece of paper, looked at it, concentrated on it, fixed it securely in his mind and then tore up the paper. In this way, he gained an eye impression of the name as well as an ear impression.

All this takes time, but 'Good manners,' said Emerson, 'are made up of petty sacrifices.'

The importance of remembering and using names is not just the prerogative of kings and corporate executives. It works for all of us. Ken Nottingham, an employee of General Motors in Indiana, usually had lunch at the company cafeteria. He noticed that the woman who worked behind the counter always had a scowl on her face. 'She had been making sandwiches for about two hours and I was just another sandwich to her. I told her what I wanted. She weighed out the ham on a little scale, then she gave me one leaf of lettuce, a few potato chips and handed them to me.

'The next day I went through the same line. Same woman, same scowl. I smiled and said, "Hello, Eunice," and then told her what I wanted. Well, she forgot the scale, piled on the ham, gave me three leaves of lettuce and heaped on the potato chips until they fell off the plate.'

We should be aware of the *magic* contained in a name and realize that this single item is wholly and completely owned by the person with whom we are dealing…and nobody else.

The name sets the individual apart; it makes him or her unique among all others. The information we are imparting or the request we are making takes on a special importance when we approach the situation with the name of the individual. From the waitress to the senior executive, the name will work magic as we deal with others.

> **POINTS TO REMEMBER**
>
> 1. The simple secret behind a person's success.
> 2. An average person is more interested in his or her own name than in all the other names on earth put together.
> 3. Opt for smart work not hard work.

3

ACQUIRING CONFIDENCE BEFORE AN AUDIENCE

Students of public speaking continually ask, 'How can I overcome self-consciousness and the fear that paralyses me before an audience?'

Did you ever notice in looking from a train window that some horses feed near the track and never even pause to look up at the thundering cars, while just ahead at the next railroad crossing, a farmer's wife will be nervously trying to quiet her scared horse as the train goes by?

How would you cure a horse that is afraid of cars—graze him in a back-woods lot where he would never see steam-engines or automobiles, or drive or pasture him where he would frequently see the machines?

Apply horse-sense to ridding yourself of self-consciousness and fear; face an audience as frequently as you can and you will soon stop shying. You can never attain freedom from stage fright by reading a treatise. A book may give you excellent suggestions on how best to conduct yourself in the water, but sooner or later you must get wet, perhaps even choke and be 'half scared to death'. There are a great many 'wetless' bathing suits worn at the seashore, but no one ever learns to swim in them. To plunge is the only way.

Practice, practice, PRACTICE in speaking before an audience will tend to remove all fear of audiences, just as practice in swimming will lead to confidence and facility in the water. You must learn to speak by speaking.

Do not be disheartened if at first you suffer from stage fright. It never hurts a fool to appear before an audience, for his capacity is not a capacity for feeling. A blow that would kill a civilized man heals soon on a savage. The higher we go in the scale of life, the greater is the capacity for suffering.

For one reason or another, some master-speakers never entirely overcome stage-fright, but it will pay you to spare no pains to conquer it. Daniel Webster failed in his first appearance and had to take his seat without finishing his speech because he was nervous. Gladstone was often troubled with self-consciousness in the beginning of an address. Beecher was always perturbed before talking in public.

Blacksmiths sometimes twist a rope tight around the nose of a horse, and by thus inflicting a little pain they distract his attention from the shoeing process. One way to get air out of a glass is to pour in water.

BE ABSORBED BY YOUR SUBJECT

Apply the blacksmith's homely principle when you are speaking. If you feel deeply about your subject you will be able to think of little else. Concentration is a process of distraction from less important matters. It is too late to think about the cut of your coat when once you are upon the platform, so centre your interest on what you are about to say—fill your mind with your speech-material and, like the infilling water in the glass, it will drive out your unsubstantial fears.

Self-consciousness is undue consciousness of self, and, for the purpose of delivery, self is secondary to your subject, not only in the opinion of the audience, but, if you are wise, in your own. To hold any other view is to regard yourself as an exhibit instead of as a messenger with a message worth delivering. It is sheer egotism to fill your mind with thoughts of self when a greater thing is there—TRUTH. Say this to yourself sternly, and shame your self-consciousness into quiescence. If the theatre caught fire you could rush to the stage and shout directions to the audience without any self-consciousness, for the importance of what you were saying would drive all fear-thoughts out of your mind.

Far worse than self-consciousness through fear of doing poorly, is self-consciousness through assumption of doing well. The first sign of greatness is when a man does not attempt to look and act great. Before you can call yourself a man at all, Kipling assures us, you must 'not look too good nor talk too wise'.

Nothing advertises itself so thoroughly as conceit. One may be so full of self as to be empty. Voltaire said, 'We must conceal self-love.' But that cannot be done. You know this to be true, for you have recognized overweening self-love in others. If you have it, others are seeing it in you. There are things in this world bigger than self, and in working for them self will be forgotten, or—what is better—remembered only so as to help us win toward higher things.

HAVE SOMETHING TO SAY

The trouble with many speakers is that they go before an audience with their minds a blank. It is no wonder that nature, abhorring a vacuum, fills them with the nearest thing handy, which generally happens to be, 'I wonder if I am doing this right! How does my hair look? I know I shall fail.' Their prophetic souls are sure to be right.

It is not enough to be absorbed by your subject—to acquire self-confidence you must have something in which to be confident. If you go before an audience without any preparation, or previous knowledge of your subject, you ought to be self-conscious—you ought to be ashamed to steal the time of your audience. Prepare yourself. Know what you are going to talk about, and, in general, how you are going to say it. Have the first few sentences worked out completely so that you may not be troubled in the beginning to find words. Know your subject better than your hearers know it, and you have nothing to fear.

AFTER PREPARING FOR SUCCESS, EXPECT IT

Let your bearing be modestly confident, but most of all, be modestly confident within. Overconfidence is bad, but to tolerate premonitions of failure is worse.

Any man who thoroughly knows himself must feel true humility; but it is not a humility that assumes a worm-like meekness; it is rather a strong, vibrant prayer for greater power for service.

Washington Irving once introduced Charles Dickens at a dinner given in the latter's honour. In the middle of his speech Irving hesitated, became embarrassed, and sat down awkwardly. Turning to a friend beside him he remarked, 'There, I told you I would fail, and I did.'

If you believe you will fail, there is no hope for you. You will.

Rid yourself of this I-am-a-poor-worm-in-the-dust idea.

You are a god, with infinite capabilities. 'All things are ready if the mind be so.' The eagle looks the cloudless sun in the face.

ASSUME MASTERY OVER YOUR AUDIENCE

In public speech, as in electricity, there is a positive and a negative force. Either you or your audience is going to possess the positive factor. If you assume it you can almost invariably make it yours. If you assume the negative you are sure to be negative. Assuming a virtue or a vice vitalizes it. Summon all your power of self-direction, and remember that though your audience is infinitely more important than you, the truth is more important than both of you, because it is eternal. If your mind falters in its leadership, the sword will drop from your hands. Your assumption of being able to instruct or lead or inspire a multitude or even a small group of people may appall you as being colossal impudence—as indeed it may be; but having once essayed to speak, be courageous. BE courageous—it lies within you to be what you will. MAKE yourself be calm and confident.

Reflect that your audience will not hurt you. In facing your audience, pause a moment and look them over—a hundred chances to one they want you to succeed, for what man is so foolish as to spend his time, perhaps his money, in the hope that you will waste his investment by talking dully?

CONCLUDING HINTS

Do not make haste to begin—haste shows lack of control.

Do not apologize. It ought not to be necessary; and if it is, it will not help. Go straight ahead.

Take a deep breath, relax, and begin in a quiet conversational tone as though you were speaking to one large friend. You will not find it half as bad as you imagined; really, it is like taking a cold plunge: after you are in, the water is fine. In fact, having spoken a few times you will even anticipate the plunge with exhilaration. To stand before an audience and make them think your thoughts after you is one of the greatest pleasures you can ever know.

So cast out fear, for fear is cowardly when it is not mastered. The bravest know fear, but they do not yield to it. Face your audience pluckily—if your knees quake, MAKE them stop. In your audience lies some victory for you and the cause you represent. Go win it. Suppose Columbus had feared to venture out into the unknown West; suppose our forefathers had been too timid to oppose the tyranny of George the Third; suppose that any man who ever did anything worthwhile had been a coward! The world owes its progress to the men who have dared, and you must dare to speak the effective word that is in your heart to speak—for often it requires courage to utter a single sentence. But remember that men erect no monuments and weave no laurels for those who fear to do what they can.

IS ALL THIS UNSYMPATHETIC, DO YOU SAY?

Man, what you need is not sympathy, but a push. No one doubts that temperament and nerves and illness and even praiseworthy modesty may, singly or combined, cause the speaker's cheek to blanch before an audience, but neither can anyone doubt that coddling will magnify this weakness. The victory lies in a fearless frame of mind. Prof. Walter Dill Scott says, 'Success or failure in business is caused more by mental attitude than by mental capacity.' Banish the fear-attitude; acquire the confident attitude. And remember that the only way to acquire it is—to acquire it.

In this foundation chapter we have tried to strike the tone of much that is to follow. Many of these ideas will be amplified and enforced in a more specific way; but through all these chapters on the art of public speaking which could even be more powerful than the public press, the note of justifiable self-confidence must come up again and again.

POINTS TO REMEMBER

1. The trick to overcome self-consciousness before an audience.
2. Practice, practice and practice.
3. The higher we go in the scale of life, the greater is the capacity for suffering.

4

FLUENCY THROUGH PREPARATION

At first blush it would seem that fluency consists in a ready, easy use of words. Not so—the flowing quality of speech is much more, for it is a composite effect, with each of its prior conditions deserving of careful notice.

THE SOURCES OF FLUENCY

Speaking broadly, fluency is almost entirely a matter of preparation. Certainly, native gifts figure largely here, as in every art, but even natural facility is dependent on the very same laws of preparation that hold good for the man of supposedly small native endowment. Let this encourage you if, like Moses, you are prone to complain that you are not a ready speaker.

Have you ever stopped to analyse that expression, 'a ready speaker'? Readiness, in its prime sense, is preparedness, and they are most ready who are best prepared. Quick firing depends more on the alert finger than on the hair trigger. Your fluency will be in direct ratio to two important conditions: your knowledge of what you are going to say, and your being accustomed to telling what you know to an audience. This gives us the second great element of fluency—to preparation must be added the ease that arises from practice; of which more presently.

KNOWLEDGE IS ESSENTIAL

Mr Bryan is a most fluent speaker when he speaks on political problems, tendencies of the time and questions of morals. It is to be supposed, however, that he would not be so fluent in speaking on the bird life of the Florida Everglades. Mr John Burroughs might be at his best on this last subject, yet entirely lost in talking about international law. Do not expect to speak fluently on a subject that you know little or nothing about. Ctesiphon boasted that he could speak all day (a sin in itself) on any subject that an audience would suggest. He was banished by the Spartans.

But preparation goes beyond the getting of the facts in the case you are to present: it includes also the ability to think and arrange your thoughts, a full and precise vocabulary, an easy manner of speech and breathing, absence of self-consciousness and the several other characteristics of efficient delivery that have deserved special attention in other parts of this book rather than in this chapter.

Preparation may be either general or specific; usually it should be both. A lifetime of reading, of companionship with stirring thoughts, of wrestling with the problems of life—this constitutes a general preparation of inestimable worth. Out of a well-stored mind, and—richer still—a broad experience, and—best of all—a warmly sympathetic heart, the speaker will have to draw much material that no immediate study could provide. General preparation consists of all that a man has put into himself, all that heredity and environment have instilled into him, and—that other rich source of preparedness for speech—the friendship of wise companions. When Schiller returned home after a visit with Goethe, a friend remarked, 'I am amazed by the progress Schiller can make within a single fortnight.' It was the progressive influence of a new friendship. Proper friendships form one of the best means for the formation of ideas and ideals, for they enable one to practice in giving expression to thought. The speaker who would speak fluently before an audience should learn to speak fluently and entertainingly with a friend. Clarify your ideas by putting them in words; the talker gains as much from his conversation as the listener. You sometimes begin to converse on a subject thinking you have very little to say, but one idea gives birth to another and you are surprised to learn that the more you give, the more you have to give. This give-and-take of friendly conversation develops mentality and fluency in expression. Longfellow said, 'A single conversation across the table with a wise man is better than ten years' study of books,' and Holmes whimsically, yet none the less truthfully, declared that half the time he talked to find out what he thought. But that method must not be applied on the platform!

After all this enrichment of life by storage, must come the special preparation for the particular speech. This is of so definite a sort that it warrants separate chapter-treatment later.

PRACTICE

But preparation must also be of another sort than the gathering, organizing and shaping of materials—it must include practice, which, like mental preparation, must be both general and special.

Do not feel surprised or discouraged if practice on the principles of delivery herein laid down seems to retard your fluency. For a time, this will be inevitable. While you are working for proper inflection, for instance, inflection will be demanding your first thoughts, and the flow of your speech, for the time being, will be secondary. This warning, however, is strictly for the closet, for your practice at home. Do not carry any thoughts of inflection with you to the platform. There you must think only of your subject. There is an absolute telepathy between the audience and the speaker. If your thought goes to your gesture, their thought will too. If your interest goes to the quality of your voice, they will be regarding that instead of what your voice is uttering.

You have doubtless been adjured to 'forget everything but your subject'. This advice says either too much or too little. The truth is that while on the platform you must not forget a great many things that are not in your subject, but you must not think of them. Your attention must consciously go only to your message, but subconsciously you will be attending to the points of technique which have become more or less habitual by practice.

A nice balance between these two kinds of attention is important.

You can no more escape this law than you can live without air: your platform gestures, your voice, your inflection, will all be just as good as your habit of gesture, voice and inflection makes them—no better. Even the thought of whether you are speaking fluently or not will have the effect of marring your flow of speech.

Return to the opening chapter on self-confidence and again lay its precepts to heart. Learn by rules to speak without thinking of rules. It is not—or ought not to be—necessary for you to stop to think how to say the alphabet correctly, as a matter of fact it is slightly more difficult for you to repeat Z, Y, X than it is to say X, Y, Z—habit has established the order. Just so you must master the laws of efficiency in speaking until it is a second nature for you to speak correctly rather than otherwise. A beginner at the piano has a great deal of trouble with the mechanics of playing, but as time goes on his fingers become trained and almost instinctively wander over the keys correctly. As an inexperienced speaker you will find a great deal of difficulty at first in putting principles into practice, for you will be scared, like the young swimmer, and make some crude strokes, but if you persevere you will 'win out.'

Thus, to sum up, the vocabulary you have enlarged by study, the ease in speaking you have developed by practice, the economy of your well-studied emphasis, all will subconsciously come to your aid on the platform. Then the habits you have formed will be earning you a splendid dividend. The fluency of your speech will be at the speed of flow your practice has made habitual.

But this means work. What good habit does not? No philosopher's stone that will act as a substitute for laborious practice has ever been found. If it were, it would be thrown away, because it would kill our greatest joy—the delight of acquisition. If public-speaking means to you a fuller life, you will know no greater happiness than a well-spoken speech. The time you have spent in gathering ideas and in private practice of speaking, you will find amply rewarded.

POINTS TO REMEMBER

1. Fluency is only a matter of preparation.
2. Proper friendships form one of the best means for the formation of ideas and ideals.
3. A balance between attention on the subject as well as the points of technique is important in a speech.

5

EARNING THE RIGHT TO TALK

"An effective speaker knows that the success or failure of his talk is not for him to decide—it will be decided in the minds and hearts of his hearers."

Many years ago, a Doctor of Philosophy and a rough-and-ready fellow who had spent his youth in the British Navy were enrolled in one of our classes in New York. The man with the degree was a college professor; the ex-tar was the proprietor of a small side-street trucking business. His talks were far better received by the class than those given by the professor. Why? The college man used beautiful English. He was urbane, cultured, refined. His talks were always logical and clear. But they lacked one essential—concreteness. They were vague and general. Not once did he illustrate a point with anything approaching a personal experience. His talks were usually nothing more than a series of abstract ideas held together by a thin string of logic.

On the other hand, the trucking firm proprietor's language was definite, concrete and picturesque. He talked in terms of everyday facts. He gave us one point and then backed it up by telling us what happened to him in the course of his business. He described the people he had to deal with and the headaches of keeping up with regulations. The virility and freshness of his phraseology made his talks highly instructive and entertaining.

I cite this instance, not because it is typical of college professors or of men in the trucking business, but because it illustrates the attention-compelling power of rich, colorful details in a talk.

There are four ways to develop speech material that guarantees audience attention. If you follow these four steps in your preparation you will be well on the way to commanding the eager attention of your listeners.

FIRST
LIMIT YOUR SUBJECT

Once you have selected your topic, the first step is to stake out the area you want to cover and stay strictly within those limits. Don't make the mistake of trying to cover the open range. One young man attempted to speak for two minutes on the subject of 'Athens from 500BC to the Korean War." How utterly futile! He barely had gone beyond the founding of the city before he had to sit down, another victim of the compulsion to cover too much in one talk. This is an extreme example, I know; I have heard thousands of talks, less encompassing in scope, that failed to hold attention for the same reason—they covered far too many points.

Why? Because it is impossible for the mind to attend to a monotonous series of factual points. If your talk sounds like the World Almanac you will not be able to hold attention very long. Take a simple subject, like a trip to Yellowstone National Park. In their eagerness to leave nothing out, most people have something to say about every scenic view in the Park. The audience is whisked from one point to another with dizzying speed. At the end, all that remains in the mind is a blur of waterfalls, mountains and geysers. How much more memorable such a talk would be if the speaker limited himself to one aspect of the Park, the wildlife or the hot springs, for example. Then there would be time to develop the kind of pictorial detail that would make Yellowstone National Park come alive in all its vivid color and variety.

This is true of any subject, whether it be salesmanship, baking cakes, tax exemptions or ballistic missiles. You must limit and select before you begin, narrow your subject down to an area that will fit the time at your disposal.

In a short talk, less than five minutes in duration, all you can expect is to get one or two main points across. In a longer talk, up to thirty minutes, few speakers ever succeed if they try to cover more than four or five main ideas.

SECOND
DEVELOP RESERVE POWER

It is far easier to give a talk that skims over the surface than to dig down for facts. But when you take the easy way you make little or no impression on the audience. After you have narrowed your subject, then the next step is to ask yourself questions that will deepen your understanding and prepare you to talk with authority on the topic you have chosen: 'Why do I believe this? When did I ever see this point exemplified in real life? What, precisely, am I trying to prove? Exactly how did it happen?'

Questions like these call for answers that will give you reserve power, the power that makes people sit up and take notice. It was said of Luther Burbank, the botanical wizard, that he produced a million plant specimens to find one or two superlative ones. It is the same with a talk. Assemble a hundred thoughts around your theme, then discard ninety.

'I always try to get ten times as much information as I use, sometimes a hundred times as much,' said John Gunther not long ago. The author of the bestselling 'Inside' books was speaking of the way he prepared to write a book or give a talk.

On one occasion in particular, his actions bore out his words. In 1956, he was working on a series of articles on mental hospitals. He visited institutions, talked to supervisors, attendants, and patients. A friend of mine was with him, giving some small assistance in the research and he told me they must have walked countless miles up stairs and down, along corridors, building to building, day after day. Mr Gunther filled notebooks. Back in his office, he stacked up government and state reports, private hospital reports and reams of committees' statistics.

'In the end,' my friend told me, 'he wrote four short articles, simple enough and anecdotal enough to make good speeches. The paper on which they were typed weighed, perhaps, a few ounces. The filled notebooks, and everything else he used as the basis for the few ounces of product, must have weighed twenty pounds.'

Mr Gunther knew that he was working with pay dirt. He knew he couldn't overlook any of it. An old hand at this sort of thing, he put his mind to it, and he sifted out the gold nuggets.

A surgeon friend of mine said, 'I can teach you in ten minutes how to take out an appendix. But it will take me four years to teach you what to do if something goes wrong.' So it is with speaking: always prepare so that you are ready for any emergency, such as a change of emphasis because of a previous speaker's remarks or a well-aimed question from the audience in the discussion period following your talk.

You, too, can acquire reserve power by selecting your topic as soon as possible. Don't put it off until a day or two before you have to speak. If you decide on the topic early you will have the inestimable advantage of having your subconscious mind working for you. At odd moments of the day when you are free from your work, you can explore your subject, refine the ideas you want to convey to your audience. Time ordinarily spent in reverie while you are driving home, waiting for a bus or riding the subway, can be devoted to mulling over the subject matter of your talk. It is during this incubation period that flashes of insight will come, just because you have determined your topic far in advance and your mind subconsciously works over it.

Norman Thomas, a superb speaker who has commanded the respectful attention of audiences quite opposed to his political point of view, said, 'If a speech is to be of any importance at all, the speaker should live with the theme or message, turning it over and over in his mind. He will be surprised at how many useful illustrations or ways of putting his case will come to him as he walks the street or reads a newspaper or gets ready for bed or wakes up in the morning. Mediocre speaking very often is merely the inevitable and the appropriate reflection of mediocre thinking, and the consequence of imperfect acquaintance with the subject in hand.'

While you are involved in this process you will be under strong temptation to write your talk out, word for word. Try not to do this, for once you have set a pattern, you are likely to be satisfied with it, and you may cease to give it any more constructive thought. In addition, there is the danger of memorizing the script. Mark Twain had this to say about such memorization, 'Written things are not for speech; their form is literary; they are stiff, inflexible, and will not lend themselves to happy effective delivery with the tongue. Where their purpose is merely to entertain, not to instruct, they have to be limbered up, broken up, colloquialized, and turned into the common form of unpremeditated talk; otherwise they will bore the house—not entertain it.'

Charles F. Kettering, whose inventive genius sparked the growth of General Motors, was one of America's most renowned and heartwarming speakers. Asked if he ever wrote out any part or all of his talks, he replied, 'What I have to say is, I believe, far too important to write down on paper. I prefer to write on my audience's mind, on their emotions, with every ounce of my being. A piece of paper cannot stand between me and those I want to impress.'

THIRD
FILL YOUR TALK WITH ILLUSTRATIONS AND EXAMPLES

In the *Art of Readable Writing,* Rudolf Flesch begins one of his chapters with this sentence, 'Only stories are really readable.' He then shows how this principle is used by *Time* and *Reader's Digest.* Almost every article in these top-circulation magazines either is written as pure narrative or is generously sprinkled with anecdotes. There is no denying the power of a story to hold attention in talking before groups as well as writing for magazines.

Norman Vincent Peale, whose sermons have been heard by millions on radio and television, says that his favorite form of supporting material in a talk is the illustration or example. He once told an interviewer from the *Quarterly Journal of Speech* that 'the true example is the finest method I know of to make an idea clear, interesting and persuasive. Usually, I use several examples to support each major point.'

Readers of my books are soon aware of my use of the

anecdote as a means of developing the main points of my message. The rules from *How to Win Friends and Influence People* can be listed on one and a half pages. The other two hundred and thirty pages of the book are filled with stories and illustrations to point up how others have used these rules with wholesome effect.

How can we acquire this most important technique of using illustrative material? There are five ways of doing this: Humanize, Personalize, Specify, Dramatize and Visualize.

HUMANIZE YOUR TALK

I once asked a group of American businessmen in Paris to talk on 'How to Succeed'. Most of them merely listed a lot of abstract qualities and gave preachments on the value of hard work, persistence and ambition.

So I halted this class, and said something like this, 'We don't want to be lectured to. No one enjoys that. Remember, you must be entertaining or we will pay no attention whatever to what you are saying. Also remember that one of the most interesting things in the world is sublimated, glorified gossip. So tell us the stories of two men you have known. Tell why one succeeded and why the other failed. We will gladly listen to that, remember it and possibly profit by it.'

There was a certain member of that course who invariably found it difficult to interest either himself or his audience. This night, however, he seized the human interest suggestion and told us of two of his classmates in college. One of them had been so conservative that he had bought shirts at the different stores in town, and made charts showing which ones laundered best, wore longest and gave the most service per dollar invested. His mind was always on pennies; yet, when he was graduated—

it was an engineering college—he had such a high opinion of his own importance that he was not willing to begin at the bottom and work his way up, as the other graduates were doing. Even when the third annual reunion of the class came, he was still making laundry charts of his shirts, while waiting for some extraordinarily good thing to come his way. It never came. A quarter of a century has passed since then, and this man, dissatisfied and soured on life, still holds a minor position.

The speaker then contrasted with this failure the story of one of his classmates who had surpassed all expectations. This particular chap was a good mixer. Everyone liked him. Although he was ambitious to do big things later, he started as a draftsman. But he was always on the lookout for opportunity. Plans were then being made for the New York World's Fair. He knew engineering talent would be needed there, so he resigned from his position in Philadelphia and moved to New York. There he formed a partnership and engaged immediately in the contracting business. They did considerable work for the telephone company, and this man was finally taken over by that concern at a large salary.

I have recorded here only the bare outline of what the speaker told. He made his talk interesting and illuminating with a score of amusing and human interest details. He talked on and on—this man who could not ordinarily find material for a three-minute speech—and he was surprised to learn, when he stopped, that he had held the floor on this occasion for ten minutes. The speech had been so interesting that it seemed short to everyone. It was his first real triumph.

Almost everyone can profit by this incident. The average speech would be far more appealing if it were rich with human interest stories. The speaker should attempt to make only a few points and to illustrate them with concrete cases. Such a method of speech building can hardly fail to get and hold attention.

Of course, the richest source of such human interest material is your own background. Don't hesitate to tell us about your experiences because of some feeling that you should not talk about yourself. The only time an audience objects to hearing a person talk about himself is when he does it in an offensive, egotistical way. Otherwise, audiences are tremendously interested in the personal stories speakers tell. They are the surest means of holding attention; don't neglect them.

PERSONALIZE YOUR TALK BY USING NAMES

By all means, when you tell stories involving others, use their names, or, if you want to protect their identity, use fictitious names. Even impersonal names like 'Mr Smith' or 'Joe Brown' are far more descriptive than 'this man' or 'a person'. The label identifies and individualizes. As Rudolf Flesch points out, 'Nothing adds more realism to a story than names; nothing is as unrealistic as anonymity. Imagine a story whose hero has no name.'

If your talk is full of names and personal pronouns you can be sure of high listenability, for you will have the priceless ingredient of human interest in your speech.

BE SPECIFIC, FILL YOUR TALK WITH DETAIL

You might say at this point, 'This is all very fine, but how can I be sure of getting enough detail into my talk?' There is one test. Use the 5-W formula every reporter follows when he writes a news story: answer the questions When? Where? Who? What? and Why? If you follow this formula your examples will have life and color. Let me illustrate this with an anecdote of my own, one that was published by the *Reader's Digest:*

'After leaving college, I spent two years traveling through South Dakota as a salesman for Armour and Company. I covered my territory by riding on freight trains. One day I had to lay over in Redfield, S. D., for two hours to get a train going south. Since Redfield was not in my territory I couldn't use the time for making sales. Within a year I was going to New York to study at the American Academy of Dramatic Arts, so I decided to use this spare time practicing speaking. I wandered down through the train yards and began rehearsing a scene for *Macbeth.* Thrusting out my arms, I cried dramatically, "Is this a dagger which I see before me, the handle toward my hand? Come, let me clutch thee: I have thee not, and yet I see thee still."

'I was still immersed in the scene when four policemen leaped upon me and asked why I was frightening women. I couldn't have been more astounded if they had accused me of robbing a train. They informed me that a housewife had been watching me from behind her kitchen curtains a hundred yards away. She had never seen such goings-on. So she called the police, and when they approached they heard me ranting about daggers.

'I told them I was "practicing Shakespeare", but I had to produce my order book for Armour and Company before they let me go.'

Notice how this anecdote answers the questions posed in the 5-W formula above.

Of course, too much detail is worse than none. All of us have been bored by lengthy recitals of superficial, irrelevant details. Notice how in the incident about my near-arrest in a South Dakota town there is a brief and concise answer to each of the 5-W questions. If you clutter your talk with too much detail, your audience will blue-pencil your remarks by refusing to give you their complete attention. There is no blue pencil more severe than inattentiveness.

DRAMATIZE YOUR TALK BY USING DIALOGUE

Suppose you want to give an illustration of how you succeeded in calming down an irate customer by using one of the rules of human relations. You could begin like this:

'The other day a man came into my office. He was pretty mad because the appliance we had sent out to his house only the week before was not working properly. I told him that we would do all we could to remedy the situation. After a while he calmed down and seemed satisfied that we had every intention to make things right.' This anecdote has one virtue—it is fairly specific—but it lacks names, specific details, and, above all, the actual dialogue which would make this incident come alive. Here it is with these added qualities:

'Last Tuesday, the door of my office slammed and I looked up to see the angry features of Charles Blexam, one of my regular customers. I didn't have time to ask him to take a seat. "Ed, this is the last straw," he said, "you can send a truck right out and cart that wash machine out of my basement."

'I asked him what was up. He was too willing to reply.

'"It won't work," he shouted, "the clothes get all tangled, and my wife's sick and tired of it."

'I asked him to sit down and explain it in more detail.

'"I haven't got time to sit down. I'm late for work and I wish I'd never come in here to buy an appliance in the first place. Believe me, I'll never do it again." Here he hit the desk with his hand and knocked over my wife's picture.

'"Look, Charley," I said, "if you will just sit down and tell me all about it, I promise to do whatever you want me to do." With that, he sat down, and we calmly talked it over.'

It isn't always possible to work dialogue into your talk, but you can see how the direct quotation of the conversation in the excerpt above helps to dramatize the incident for the listener. If the speaker has some imitative skill and can get the original tone of voice into the words, dialogue can become more effective. Also, dialogue gives your speech the authentic ring of everyday conversation. It makes you sound like a real person talking across a dinner table, not like a pedant delivering a paper before a learned society or an orator ranting into a microphone.

VISUALIZE BY DEMONSTRATING WHAT YOU ARE TALKING ABOUT

Psychologists tell us that more than 85 per cent of our knowledge comes to us through visual impressions. No doubt this accounts for the enormous effectiveness of television as an advertising as well as entertainment medium. Public speaking, too, is a visual as well as auditory art.

One of the best ways to enrich a talk with detail is to incorporate visual demonstration into it. You might spend hours just telling me how to swing a golf club, and I might be bored by it. But get up and show me what you do when you drive a ball down the fairway and I am all eyes and ears. Likewise, if you describe the erratic maneuvers of an airplane with your arms and shoulders, I am more intent on the outcome of your brush with death.

I remember a talk given in an industrial class that was a masterpiece of visual detail. The speaker was poking good-natured fun at inspectors and efficiency experts. His mimicry of the gestures and bodily antics of these gentlemen as they inspected a broken-down machine was more hilarious than anything I have ever seen on television. What is more, visual detail made that talk memorable—I for one shall never forget it, and I am sure the other members of that class are still talking about it.

It is a good idea to ask yourself, 'How can I put some visual detail into my talk?' Then proceed to demonstrate, for, as the ancient Chinese observed, one picture is worth ten thousand words.

FOURTH
USE CONCRETE, FAMILIAR WORDS THAT CREATE PICTURES

In the process of getting and holding attention, which is the first purpose of every speaker, there is one aid, one technique, that is of the highest importance. Yet, it is all but ignored. The average speaker does not seem to be aware of its existence. He has probably never consciously thought about it at all. I refer to the process of using words that create pictures. The speaker who is easy to listen to is the one who sets images floating before your eyes. The one who employs foggy, commonplace, colorless symbols sets the audience to nodding.

Pictures, Pictures. Pictures. They are as free as the air you breathe. Sprinkle them through your talks, your conversation, and you will be more entertaining, more influential.

Herbert Spencer, in his famous essay on the 'Philosophy of Style', pointed out long ago the superiority of terms that call forth bright pictures:

'We do not think in generals but in particulars… We should avoid such a sentence as:

"'In proportion as the manners, customs and amusements

of a nation are cruel and barbarous, the regulations of their penal code will be severe!"

'And in place of it, we should write:

'"In proportion as men delight in battles, bull fights and combats of gladiators, will they punish by hanging, burning and the rack."'

Picture-building phrases swarm through the pages of the Bible and through Shakespeare like bees around a cider mill. For example, a commonplace writer would have said that a certain thing would be 'superfluous', like trying to improve the perfect. How did Shakespeare express the same thought? With a picture phrase that is immortal, 'To gild refined gold, to paint the lily, to throw perfume on the violet.'

Did you ever pause to observe that the proverbs that are passed on from generation to generation are almost all visual sayings? 'A bird in the hand is worth two in the bush.' 'It never rains but it pours.' 'You can lead a horse to water but you can't make him drink.' And you will find the same picture element in almost all the similes that have lived for centuries and grown hoary with too much use: 'sly as a fox', 'dead as a doornail', 'flat as a pancake', 'hard as a rock'.

Lincoln continually talked in visual terminology. When he became annoyed with the long, complicated, red-tape reports that came to his desk in the White House, he objected to them, not with colorless phraseology, but with a picture phrase that it is almost impossible to forget. 'When I send a man to buy a horse,' he said, 'I don't want to be told how many hairs the horse has in his tail. I wish only to know his points.'

Make your eye appeals definite and specific. Paint mental pictures that stand out as sharp and clear as a stag's antlers silhouetted against the setting sun. For example, the word 'dog' calls up a more or less definite picture of such an animal—

perhaps a cocker spaniel, a Scottish terrier, a St. Bernard or a Pomeranian. Notice how much more distinct an image springs into your mind when a speaker says 'bulldog'—the term is less inclusive. Doesn't 'a brindle bulldog' call up a still more explicit picture? Is it not more vivid to say 'a black Shetland pony' than to talk of 'a horse'? Doesn't 'a white bantam rooster with a broken leg' give a much more definite and sharper picture than merely the word 'fowl'?

In *The Elements of Style,* William Strunk, Jr., states, 'If those who have studied the art of writing are in accord on any one point, it is on this: the surest way to arouse and hold the attention of the reader is by being specific, definit' and concrete. The greatest writers—Homer, Dante, Shakespeare—are effective largely because they deal in particulars and report the details that matter. Their words call up pictures." This is as true of speaking as of writing.

I once devoted a session years ago in my course in Effective Speaking to an experiment in being factual. We adopted a rule that in every sentence the speaker must put either a fact or a proper noun, a figure or a date. The results were revolutionary. The class members made a game of catching one another on generalities; it wasn't long before they were talking, not the cloudy language that floats over the head of an audience, but the clear-cut, vigorous language of the man on the street.

'An abstract style,' said the French philosopher Alain, 'is always bad. Your sentences should be full of stones, metals, chairs, tables, animals, men and women.'

This is true of everyday conversation as well. In fact, all that has been said in this chapter about the use of detail in talks before groups applies to general conversation. It is detail that makes conversation sparkle. Anyone who is intent upon making himself a more effective conversationalist may profit by following the advice contained in this chapter. Salesmen, too, will discover the magic of detail when applied to their sales presentations. Those in executive positions, housewives and teachers will find that giving instructions and dispensing information will be greatly improved by the use of concrete, factual detail.

POINTS TO REMEMBER

1. Instead of covering every point, stick to a few points and concisely explain them.
2. It's better to speak in anecdotal form to gain effectiveness and rapt-attention.
3. Don't be abstract. It is boring.

6

VITALIZING THE TALK

Right after the First World War, I was in London working with Lowell Thomas, who was giving a series of brilliant lectures on Allenby and Lawrence of Arabia to packed houses. One Sunday I wandered into Hyde Park to the spot near the Marble Arch entrance where speakers of every creed, color, and political and religious persuasion are allowed to air their views without interference from the law. For a while I listened to a Catholic explaining the doctrine of the infallibility of the Pope, then I moved to the fringes of another crowd, intent upon what a Socialist had to say about Karl Marx. I strolled over to a third speaker, who was explaining why it was right and proper for a man to have four wives! Then I moved away and looked back at the three groups.

Would you believe it? The man who was talking about polygamy had the fewest number of people listening to him! There was only a handful. The crowds around the other two speakers were growing larger by the minute. I asked myself why? Was it the disparity of topics? I don't think so. The explanation, I saw as I watched, was to be found in the speakers themselves. The fellow who was talking about the advantages of having four wives didn't seem to be interested in having four wives himself. But the other two speakers, talking from almost diametrically opposed points of view, were wrapped up in their subjects. They talked with life and spirit. Their arms moved in impassioned gestures. Their voices rang with conviction. They radiated earnestness and animation.

Vitality, aliveness, enthusiasm—these are the first qualities I have always considered essential in a speaker. People cluster around the energetic speaker like wild turkeys around a field of autumn wheat.

How do you acquire this vital delivery that will keep the attention of your audience? In the course of this chapter I will give you three sovereign ways to help you put enthusiasm and excitement into your speaking.

FIRST
CHOOSE SUBJECTS YOU ARE EARNEST ABOUT

In Chapter Three was stressed the importance of feeling deeply about your subject. Unless you are emotionally involved in the subject matter you have chosen to talk about, you cannot expect to make your audience believe in your message. Obviously, if you select a topic that is exciting to you because of long experience with it, such as a hobby or recreational pursuit, or because of deep reflection or personal concern about it (as, for instance, the need for better schools in your community), you will have no difficulty in talking with excitement. The persuasive power of earnestness was never more vividly demonstrated to me than in a talk made before one of my classes in New York City more than two decades ago. I have heard many persuasive talks, but this one, which I call the Case of Blue Grass vs. Hickory Wood Ashes, stands out as a kind of triumph of sincerity over common sense.

A top-flight salesman of one of the best-known selling

organizations in the city made the preposterous statement that he had been able to make blue grass grow without the aid of seeds or roots. He had, according to his story, scattered hickory wood ashes over newly plowed ground. Presto! Blue grass had appeared! He firmly believed that the hickory wood ashes, and the hickory wood ashes alone, were responsible for the blue grass.

Commenting on his talk, I gently pointed out to him that his phenomenal discovery would, if true, make him a millionaire, for blue grass seed was worth several dollars a bushel. I also told him that it would make him the outstanding scientist of all history. I informed him that no man, living or dead, had ever been able to perform the miracle he claimed to have performed: no man had ever been able to produce life from inert matter.

I told him that very quietly, for I felt that his mistake was so palpable, so absurd, as to require no emphasis in the refutation. When I had finished, every other member of the course saw the folly of his assertion; but he did not see it, not for a second. He was in earnest about his contention, deadly in earnest. He leaped to his feet and informed me that he was *not* wrong. He had not been relating theory, he protested, but personal experience. He *knew* whereof he spoke. He continued to talk, enlarging on his first remarks, giving additional information, piling up additional evidence, sincerity and honesty ringing in his voice.

Again I informed him that there was not the remotest hope in the world of his being right or even approximately right or within a thousand miles of the truth. In a second he was on his feet once more, offering to bet me five dollars and to let the U. S. Department of Agriculture settle the matter.

And do you know what happened? Several members in the

class were won over to his side. Many others were beginning to be doubtful. If I had taken a vote I am certain that more than half of the businessmen in that class would not have sided with me. I asked them what had shaken them from their original position. One after another said it was the speaker's earnestness, his belief, so energetically stated, that made them begin to doubt the common-sense viewpoint.

Well, in the face of that display of credulity I had to write the Department of Agriculture. I was ashamed, I told them, to ask such an absurd question. They replied, of course, that it was impossible to get blue grass or any other living thing from hickory wood ashes, and they added that they had received another letter from New York asking the same question. That salesman was so sure of his position that he sat down and wrote a letter, too!

This incident taught me a lesson I'll never forget. *If a speaker believes a thing earnestly enough and says it earnestly enough, he will get adherents to his cause,* even though he claims he can produce blue grass from dust and ashes. How much more compelling will our convictions be if they are arrayed on the side of common sense and truth!

Almost all speakers wonder whether the topic they have chosen will interest the audience. There is only one way to make sure that they will be interested: stoke the fires of your enthusiasm for the subject and you will have no difficulty holding the interest of a group of people.

A short time ago, I heard a man in one of our classes in Baltimore warn his audience that if the present methods of catching rock fish in Chesapeake Bay were continued the species would become extinct. And in a very few years! He felt his subject. It was important. He was in real earnest about it. Everything about his matter and manner showed that. When he arose to speak, I did not know that there was such a creature as a rock fish in Chesapeake Bay. I imagine that more of the audience shared my lack of knowledge and lack of interest. But before the speaker finished, all of us would probably have been willing to sign a petition to the legislature to protect the rock fish by law.

Richard Washburn Child, the former American Ambassador to Italy, was once asked the secret of his success as an interesting writer. He replied, 'I am so excited about life that I cannot keep still. I just have to tell people about it.' One cannot keep from being enthralled with a speaker or writer like that.

I once went to hear a speaker in London; after he was through, one of our party, Mr E. F. Benson, a well-known English novelist, remarked that he enjoyed the last part of the talk far more than the first. When I asked him why, he replied, 'The speaker himself seemed more interested in the last part, and I always rely on the speaker to supply the enthusiasm and interest.'

Here is another illustration of the importance of choosing your topics well.

A gentleman, whom we shall call Mr Flynn, was enrolled in one of our classes in Washington, D. C. One evening early in the course, he devoted his talk to a description of the capital city of the United States. He had hastily and superficially gleaned his facts from a booklet issued by a local newspaper. They sounded like it—dry, disconnected, undigested. Though he had lived in Washington for many years, he did not present one personal instance of why he liked the city. He merely recited a series of dull facts, and his talk was as distressing for the class to hear as it was agonizing for him to give.

A fortnight later, something happened that touched Mr Flynn to the core: an unknown driver had smashed into his new car while it was parked on the street and had driven away without identifying himself. It was impossible for Mr Flynn to collect insurance and he had to foot the bill himself. Here was something that came hot out of his experience. His talk about the city of Washington, which he laboriously pulled out sentence by sentence, was painful to him and his audience; but when he spoke about his smashed-up car, his talk welled up and boiled forth like Vesuvius in action. The same class that had squirmed restlessly in their seats two weeks before now greeted Mr Flynn with a heart-warming burst of applause.

As I have pointed out repeatedly, you cannot help but succeed if you choose the right topic for you. One area of topics is sure-fire: talk about your convictions! Surely you have strong beliefs about some aspect of life around you. You don't have to search far and wide for these subjects—they generally lie on the surface of your stream of consciousness, because you often think about them.

Not long ago, a legislative hearing on capital punishment was presented on television. Many witnesses were called to give their viewpoints on both sides of this controversial subject. One of them was a member of the police department of the city of Los Angeles, who had evidently given much thought to this topic. He had strong convictions based on the fact that eleven of his fellow police officers had been killed in gun battles with criminals. He spoke with the deep sincerity of one who believed to his heart's core in the righteousness of his cause. The greatest appeals in the history of eloquence have all been made out of the depths of someone's deep convictions and feelings. Sincerity rests upon belief, and belief is as much a matter of the heart and of warmly feeling what you are saying as it is of the mind and coldly thinking of what to say. 'The heart has reasons that the reason does not know.' In many classes I have had frequent occasions to verify Pascal's trenchant sentence.

I remember a lawyer in Boston who was blessed with a striking appearance and who spoke with admirable fluency, but when he finished speaking people said, "Clever chap." He made a surface impression because there never seemed to be any feeling behind his glittering facade of words. In the same class, there was an insurance salesman, small in stature, unprepossessing in appearance, a man who groped for a word now and then, but when he spoke there was no doubt in any of his listeners' minds that he felt every word of his talk. It is almost a hundred years since Abraham Lincoln's assassination in the presidential box of Ford's Theatre in Washington, D. C., but the deep sincerity of his life and his words still lives with us. As far as knowledge of law is concerned, scores of other men of his time outstripped him. He lacked grace, smoothness and polish. But the honesty and sincerity of his utterances at Gettysburg, Cooper Union, and on the steps of the Capitol in Washington, have not been surpassed in our history.

You may say, as one man once did, that you have no strong convictions or interests. I am always a little surprised at this, but I told this man to get busy and get interested in something. 'What, for instance?' he asked. In desperation I said, 'Pigeons.' 'Pigeons?' he asked in a bewildered tone. 'Yes,' I told him, 'pigeons. Go out on the square and look at them, feed them, go to the library and read about them, then come back here and talk about them.' He did. When he came back there was no holding him down. He started to talk about pigeons with all the fervor of a fancier. When I tried to stop him he was saying something about forty books on pigeons and he had read them all. He gave one of the most interesting talks I have ever heard.

Here is another suggestion: learn more and more about what you now consider a pretty good topic. The more you know about something the more earnest and excitedly enthusiastic you will become. Percy H. Whiting, the author of the *Five Great Rules of Selling*, tells salesmen never to stop learning about the product they are selling. As Mr Whiting says, 'The more you know about a good product, the more enthusiastic you become about it.' The same thing is true about your topics—the more you know about them, the more earnest and enthusiastic you will be about them.

SECOND
RELIVE THE FEELINGS YOU HAVE ABOUT YOUR TOPIC

Suppose you are telling your audience about the policeman who stopped you for going one mile over the speed limit. You can tell us that with all the cool disinterestedness of an onlooker, but it happened to you and you had certain feelings which you expressed in quite definite language. The third-person approach will not make much of an impression on your audience. They want to know exactly how you felt when that policeman wrote out that ticket. So, the more you relive the scene you are describing, or recreate the emotions you felt originally, the more vividly you will express yourself.

One of the reasons why we go to plays and movies is that we want to hear and see emotions expressed. We have become so fearful of giving vent to our feelings in public that we have to go to a play to satisfy this need for emotional expression.

When you speak in public, therefore, you will generate excitement and interest in your talk in proportion to the amount of excitement you put into it. Don't repress your honest feelings; don't put a damper on your authentic enthusiasms. Show your listeners how eager you are to talk about your subject, and you will hold their attention.

THIRD
ACT IN EARNEST

When you walk before your audience to speak, do so with an air of anticipation, not like a man who is ascending the gallows. The spring in your walk may be largely put on, but it will do wonders for you and it gives the audience the feeling that you have something you are eager to talk about. Just before you begin, take a deep breath. Keep away from furniture or from the speaker's stand. Keep your head high and your chin up. You are about to tell your listeners something worthwhile, and every part of you should inform them of that clearly and unmistakably. You are in command, and as William James would say, act as if you are. If you make an effort to send your voice to the back of the hall, the sound will reassure you. Once you begin making gestures of any kind, they will help to stimulate you.

This principle of 'warming up our reactivity', as Donald and Eleanor Laird describe it, can be applied to all situations that demand mental awareness. In their book *Techniques for Efficient Remembering*, the Lairds point to President Theodore Roosevelt as a man who 'breezed through life with a bounce, vigor, dash and enthusiasm which became his trademark. He was absorbingly interested, or effectively pretended he was, in everything he tackled.' Teddy Roosevelt was a living exponent of the philosophy of William James, 'Act in earnest and you will become naturally earnest in all you do.'

Above all, remember this: acting in earnest will make you feel earnest.

POINTS TO REMEMBER

1. Develop interest in your subject.
2. Vitality, aliveness, enthusiasm—are the qualities essential in a speaker.
3. If a speaker believes a thing earnestly enough and says it earnestly enough, he will get adherents to his cause.

7

INFLUENCING THE CROWD

In the early part of July, 1914, a collection of Frenchmen in Paris, or Germans in Berlin, was not a crowd in a psychological sense. Each individual had his own special interests and needs, and there was no powerful common idea to unify them. A group then represented only a collection of individuals. A month later, any collection of Frenchmen or Germans formed a crowd: patriotism, hate, a common fear, a pervasive grief, had unified the individuals.

The psychology of the crowd is far different from the psychology of the personal members that compose it. The crowd is a distinct entity. Individuals restrain and subdue many of their impulses at the dictates of reason. The crowd never reasons. It only feels. As persons there is a sense of responsibility attached to our actions which checks many of our incitements, but the sense of responsibility is lost in the crowd because of its numbers. The crowd is exceedingly suggestible and will act upon the wildest and most extreme ideas. The crowd-mind is primitive and will cheer plans and perform actions which its members would utterly repudiate.

A mob is only a highly-wrought crowd. Ruskin's description is fitting, 'You can talk a mob into anything; its feelings may be—usually are—on the whole, generous and right, but it has no foundation for them, no hold of them. You may tease or tickle it into anything at your pleasure. It thinks by infection, for the most part, catching an opinion like a cold, and there is nothing so little that it will not roar itself wild about, when the fit is on, nothing so great but it will forget in an hour when the fit is past.'

History will show us how the crowd-mind works. The medieval mind was not given to reasoning; the medieval man attached great weight to the utterance of authority; his religion touched chiefly the emotions. These conditions provided a rich soil for the propagation of the crowd-mind when, in the eleventh century, flagellation, a voluntary self-scourging, was preached by the monks. Substituting flagellation for reciting penitential psalms was advocated by the reformers. A scale was drawn up, making one thousand strokes equivalent to ten psalms, or fifteen thousand to the entire psalter. This craze spread by leaps—and crowds. Flagellant fraternities sprang up. Priests carrying banners led through the streets great processions reciting prayers and whipping their bloody bodies with leathern thongs fitted with four iron points. Pope Clement denounced this practice and several of the leaders of these processions had to be burned at the stake before the frenzy could be uprooted.

All Western and Central Europe was turned into a crowd by the preaching of the crusaders, and millions of the followers of the Prince of Peace rushed to the Holy Land to kill the heathen. Even the children started on a crusade against the Saracens. The mob-spirit was so strong that home affections and persuasion could not prevail against it and thousands of mere babes died in their attempts to reach and redeem the Sacred Sepulchre.

In the early part of the eighteenth century the South Sea Company was formed in England. Britain became a speculative crowd. Stock in the South Sea Company rose from 128-1/2 points in January to 550 in May, and scored 1,000 in July. Five million shares were sold at this premium. Speculation ran riot. Hundreds of companies were organized. One was formed 'for a wheel of perpetual motion'. Another never troubled to give any reason at all for taking the cash of its subscribers—it merely announced that it was organized 'for a design which will hereafter be promulgated'. Owners began to sell, the mob caught the suggestion, a panic ensued, the South Sea Company stock fell 800 points in a few days and more than a billion dollars evaporated in this era of frenzied speculation.

The burning of the witches at Salem, the Klondike gold craze and the forty-eight people who were killed by mobs in the United States in 1913, are examples familiar to us.

THE CROWD MUST HAVE A LEADER

The leader of the crowd or mob is its determining factor. He becomes self-hynoptized with the idea that unifies its members, his enthusiasm is contagious—and so is theirs. The crowd acts as he suggests. The great mass of people do not have any very sharply-drawn conclusions on any subject outside of their own little spheres, but when they become a crowd they are perfectly willing to accept ready-made, hand-me-down opinions. They will follow a leader at all costs—in labour troubles they often follow a leader in preference to obeying their government, in war they will throw self-preservation to the bushes and follow a leader in the face of guns that fire fourteen times a second. The mob becomes shorn of will-power and blindly obedient to its dictator. The Russian Government, recognizing the menace of the crowd-mind to its autocracy, formerly prohibited public gatherings. History is full of similar instances.

HOW THE CROWD IS CREATED

Today the crowd is as real a factor in our socialized life as are magnates and monopolies. It is too complex a problem merely to damn or praise it—it must be reckoned with, and mastered. The present problem is how to get the most and the best out of the crowd-spirit, and the public speaker finds this to be peculiarly his own question. His influence is multiplied if he can only transmute his audience into a crowd. His affirmations must be their conclusions.

This can be accomplished by unifying the minds and needs of the audience and arousing their emotions. Their feelings, not their reason, must be played upon—it is 'up to' him to do this nobly. Argument has its place on the platform, but even its potencies must subserve the speaker's plan of attack to win possession of his audience.

Read the chapter on Feeling and Enthusiasm. It is impossible to make an audience a crowd without appealing to their emotions. Can you imagine the average group becoming a crowd while hearing a lecture on Dry Fly Fishing or on Egyptian Art? On the other hand, it would not have required world-famous eloquence to have turned any audience in Ulster, in 1914, into a crowd by discussing the Home Rule Act. The crowd-spirit depends largely on the subject used to fuse their individualities into one glowing whole.

To unify single auditors into a crowd, express their common needs, aspirations, dangers and emotions, deliver your message so that the interests of one shall appear to be the interests of all. The conviction of one man is intensified in proportion as he finds others sharing his belief—and feeling.

Applause, generally a sign of feeling, helps to unify an audience. The nature of the crowd is illustrated by the contagion of applause. Recently a throng in a New York moving-picture and vaudeville house had been applauding several songs, and when an advertisement for tailored skirts was thrown on the screen someone started the applause, and the crowd, like sheep, blindly imitated—until someone saw the joke and laughed; then the crowd again followed a leader and laughed at and applauded its own stupidity.

Actors sometimes start applause for their lines by snapping their fingers. Someone in the first few rows will mistake it for faint applause and the whole theatre will chime in.

An observant auditor will be interested in noticing the various devices a monologist will use to get the first round of laughter and applause. He works so hard because he knows an audience of units is an audience of indifferent critics, but once get them to laughing together and each single laughter sweeps a number of others with him, until the whole theatre is aroar and the entertainer has scored. These are meretricious schemes, to be sure, and do not savour in the least of inspiration, but crowds have not changed in their nature in a thousand years and the one law holds for the greatest preacher and the pettiest stump-speaker—you must fuse your audience, or they will not warm to your message. The devices of the great orator may not be so obvious as those of the vaudeville monologist, but the principle is the same: he tries to strike some universal note that will have all his hearers feeling alike at the same time.

The evangelist knows this when he has the soloist sing some touching song just before the address. Or he will have the entire congregation sing, and that is the psychology of 'Now everybody sing!' for he knows that they who will not join in the song are as yet outside the crowd. Many a time has the popular evangelist stopped in the middle of his talk, when he felt that his hearers were units instead of a molten mass (and a sensitive speaker can feel that condition most depressingly) and suddenly demanded that everyone arise and sing, or repeat aloud a familiar passage, or read in unison; or perhaps he has subtly left the thread of his discourse to tell a story that, from long experience, he knew would not fail to bring his hearers to a common feeling.

These things are important resources for the speaker, and happy is he who uses them worthily and not as a despicable charlatan. The difference between a demagogue and a leader is not so much a matter of method as of principle. Even the most dignified speaker must recognize the eternal laws of human nature. You are by no means urged to become a trickster on the platform—far from it—but don't kill your speech with dignity. To be icily correct is as silly as to rant. Do neither, but appeal to those world-old elements in your audience that have been recognized by all great speakers from Demosthenes to Sam Small, and see to it that you never debase your powers by arousing your hearers unworthily.

It is as hard to kindle enthusiasm in a scattered audience as to build a fire with scattered sticks. An audience to be converted into a crowd must be made to appear as a crowd. This cannot be done when they are widely scattered over a large seating space or when many empty benches separate the speaker from his hearers. Have your audience seated compactly. How many a preacher has bemoaned the enormous edifice over which what would normally be a large congregation has scattered in chilled and chilling solitude Sunday after Sunday! Bishop Brooks himself could not have inspired a congregation of one thousand souls seated in the vastness of St. Peter's at Rome. In that colossal sanctuary it is only on great occasions which bring out the multitudes that the service is before the high altar—at other times the smaller side-chapels are used.

Universal ideas surcharged with feeling help to create the crowd-atmosphere. Examples: liberty, character, righteousness, courage, fraternity, altruism, country and national heroes. George Cohan was making psychology practical and profitable when he introduced the flag and flag-songs into his musical comedies. Cromwell's regiments prayed before the battle and went into the fight singing hymns. The French corps, singing the Marseillaise in 1914, charged the Germans as one man. Such unifying devices arouse the feelings, make soldiers fanatical mobs—and, alas, more efficient murderers.

POINTS TO REMEMBER

1. Reality behind mob-mentality.
2. The leader of the crowd or mob is its determining factor.
3. Applause, generally a sign of feeling, helps to unify an audience.

8

THE VOICE

> *'Your purpose is to make your audience see what you saw, hear what you heard, feel what you felt. Relevant detail, couched in concrete, colorful language, is the best way to recreate the incident as it happened and to picture it for the audience.'*

The dramas critic of *The London Times* once declared that acting is nine-tenths voice work. Leaving the message aside, the same may justly be said of public speaking. A rich, correctly-used voice is the greatest physical factor of persuasiveness and power, often over-topping the effects of reason.

But a good voice, well handled, is not only an effective possession for the professional speaker, it is a mark of personal culture as well, and even a distinct commercial asset. Gladstone, himself the possessor of a deep, musical voice, has said, 'Ninety men in every hundred in the crowded professions will probably never rise above mediocrity because the training of the voice is entirely neglected and considered of no importance.' These are words worth pondering.

There are three fundamental requisites for a good voice:

1. Ease

Signor Bonci of the Metropolitan Opera Company says that the secret of good voice is relaxation; and this is true, for relaxation is the basis of ease. The air waves that produce voice result in a different kind of tone when striking against relaxed muscles than when striking constricted muscles. Try this for yourself. Contract the muscles of your face and throat as you do in hate, and flame out 'I hate you!' Now relax as you do when thinking gentle, tender thoughts, and say, 'I love you.' How different the voice sounds.

In practising voice exercises, and in speaking, never force your tones. Ease must be your watchword. The voice is a delicate instrument, and you must not handle it with hammer and tongs. Don't make your voice go—let it go. Don't work. Let the yoke of speech be easy and its burden light.

Your throat should be free from strain during speech, therefore it is necessary to avoid muscular contraction. The throat must act as a sort of chimney or funnel for the voice, hence any unnatural constriction will not only harm its tones but injure its health.

Nervousness and mental strain are common sources of mouth and throat constriction, so make the battle for poise and self-confidence for which we pleaded in the opening chapter.

'But how can I relax?' you ask. By simply willing to relax. Hold your arm out straight from your shoulder. Now—withdraw all power and let it fall. Practice relaxation of the muscles of the throat by letting your neck and head fall forward. Roll the upper part of your body around, with the waist line acting as a pivot. Let your head fall and roll around as you shift the torso to different positions. Do not force your head around—simply relax your neck and let gravity pull it around as your body moves.

Again, let your head fall forward on your breast; raise your head, letting your jaw hang. Relax until your jaw feels heavy, as though it were a weight hung to your face. Remember, you must relax the jaw to obtain command of it. It must be free and flexible for the moulding of tone, and to let the tone pass out unobstructed.

The lips also must be made flexible, to aid in the moulding of clear and beautiful tones. For flexibility of lips repeat the syllables, mo—me. In saying mo, bring the lips up to resemble the shape of the letter O. In repeating me draw them back as you do in a grin. Repeat this exercise rapidly, giving the lips as much exercise as possible.

Try the following exercise in the same manner:

Mo—E—O—E—OO—Ah.

After this exercise has been mastered, the following will also be found excellent for flexibility of lips:

Memorize these sounds indicated (not the expressions) so that you can repeat them rapidly.

A	as in	May.	E	as in	Met.	U	as in	Use.
A	"	Ah.	I	"	Ice.	Oi	"	Oil.
A	"	At.	I	"	It.	u	"	Our.
O	"	No.	O	"	No.	O	"	Ooze.
A	"	All.	OO	"	Foot.	A	"	Ah.
E	"	Eat.	OO	"	Ooze.	E	"	Eat.

All the activity of breathing must be centred, not in the throat, but in the middle of the body—you must breathe from the diaphragm. Note the way you breathe when lying flat on the back, undressed in bed. You will observe that all the activity then centres around the diaphragm. This is the natural and correct method of breathing. By constant watchfulness make this your habitual manner, for it will enable you to relax more perfectly the muscles of the throat.

The next fundamental requisite for good voice is openness.

2. Openness

If the muscles of the throat are constricted, the tone passage partially closed and the mouth kept half-shut, how can you expect the tone to come out bright and clear, or even to come out at all? Sound is a series of waves, and if you make a prison of your mouth, holding the jaws and lips rigidly, it will be very difficult for the tone to squeeze through, and even when it does escape it will lack force and carrying power. Open your mouth wide, relax all the organs of speech, and let the tone flow out easily.

Start to yawn, but instead of yawning, speak while your throat is open. Make this open-feeling habitual when speaking—we say make because it is a matter of resolution and of practice, if your vocal organs are healthy. Your tone passages may be partly closed by enlarged tonsils, adenoids, or enlarged turbinate bones of the nose. If so, a skilled physician should be consulted.

The nose is an important tone passage and should be kept open and free for perfect tones. What we call 'talking through the nose' is not talking through the nose, as you can easily demonstrate by holding your nose as you talk. If you are bothered with nasal tones caused by growths or swellings in the nasal passages, a slight, painless operation will remove the obstruction. This is quite important, aside from voice, for the general health will be much lowered if the lungs are continually starved for air.

The final fundamental requisite for good voice is:

3. Forwardness

A voice that is pitched back in the throat is dark, sombre and unattractive. The tone must be pitched forward, but do not force it forward. You will recall that our first principle was ease. Think the tone forward and out. Believe it is going forward, and allow it to flow easily. You can tell whether you are placing your tone forward or not by inhaling a deep breath and singing ah with the mouth wide open, trying to feel the little delicate sound waves strike the bony arch of the mouth just above the front teeth. The sensation is so slight that you will probably not be able to detect it at once, but persevere in your practice, always thinking the tone forward, and you will be rewarded by feeling your voice strike the roof of your mouth. A correct forward-placing of the tone will do away with the dark, throaty tones that are so unpleasant, inefficient and harmful to the throat.

Close the lips, humming ng, im or an. Think the tone forward. Do you feel it strike the lips?

Hold the palm of your hand in front of your face and say vigorously 'crash, dash, whirl, buzz'. Can you feel the forward tones strike against your hand? Practice until you can. Remember, the only way to get your voice forward is to put it forward.

HOW TO DEVELOP THE CARRYING POWER OF THE VOICE

It is not necessary to speak loudly in order to be heard at a distance. It is necessary only to speak correctly. Edith Wynne Matthison's voice will carry in a whisper throughout a large theatre. A paper rustling on the stage of a large auditorium can be heard distinctly in the furthermost seat in the gallery. If you will only use your voice correctly, you will not have much difficulty in being heard. Of course, it is always well to address your speech to your furthest auditors; if they get it, those nearer will have no trouble, but aside from this obvious suggestion, you must observe these laws of voice production:

Remember to apply the principles of ease, openness and forwardness—they are the prime factors in enabling your voice to be heard at a distance.

Do not gaze at the floor as you talk. This habit not only gives the speaker an amateurish appearance but if the head is hung forward the voice will be directed towards the ground instead of floating out over the audience.

Voice is a series of air vibrations. To strengthen it two things are necessary: more air or breath and more vibration.

Breath is the very basis of voice. As a bullet with little powder behind it will not have force and carrying power, so the voice that has little breath behind it will be weak. Not only will deep breathing—breathing from the diaphragm—give the voice a better support, but it will give it a stronger resonance by improving the general health.

Usually, ill health means a weak voice, while abundant physical vitality is shown through a strong, vibrant voice. Therefore, anything that improves the general vitality is an excellent voice strengthener, provided you use the voice properly. Authorities differ on most of the rules of hygiene but on one point they all agree: vitality and longevity are increased by deep breathing. Practice this until it becomes second nature. Whenever you are speaking, take in deep breaths, but in such a manner that the inhalations will be silent.

Do not try to speak too long without renewing your breath. Nature cares for this pretty well unconsciously in conversation, and she will do the same for you in platform speaking if you do not interfere with her premonitions.

A certain very successful speaker developed voice carrying power by running across country, practising his speeches as he went. The vigorous exercise forced him to take deep breaths and developed lung power. A hard-fought basketball or tennis game is an efficient way of practising deep breathing. When these methods are not convenient, we recommend the following:

Place your hands at your sides, on the waist line.

By trying to encompass your waist with your fingers and thumbs, force all the air out of the lungs.

Take a deep breath. Remember, all the activity is to be centred in the middle of the body; do not raise the shoulders. As the breath is taken your hands will be forced out.

Repeat the exercise, placing your hands on the small of the back and forcing them out as you inhale.

Many methods for deep breathing have been given by various authorities. Get the air into your lungs—that is the important thing.

The body acts as a sounding board for the voice just as the body of the violin acts as a sounding board for its tones. You can increase its vibrations by practice.

Place your finger on your lip and hum the musical scale, thinking and placing the voice forward on the lips. Do you feel the lips vibrate? After a little practice they will vibrate, giving a tickling sensation.

Repeat this exercise, throwing the humming sound into the nose. Hold the upper part of the nose between the thumb and forefinger. Can you feel the nose vibrate?

Placing the palm of your hand on top of your head, repeat this humming exercise. Think the voice there as you hum in head tones. Can you feel the vibration there?

Now place the palm of your hand on the back of your

head, repeating the foregoing process. Then try it on the chest. Always remember to think your tone where you desire to feel the vibrations. The mere act of thinking about any portion of your body will tend to make it vibrate.

Repeat the following, after a deep inhalation, endeavouring to feel all portions of your body vibrate at the same time. When you have attained this, you will find that it is a pleasant sensation.

What ho, my jovial mates! Come on! We will frolic like fairies, frisking in the merry moonshine.

PURITY OF VOICE

This quality is sometimes destroyed by wasting the breath. Carefully control the breath, using only as much as is necessary for the production of tone. Utilize all that you give out. Failure to do this results in a breathy tone. Take in breaths like a prodigal; in speaking, give it out like a miser.

VOICE SUGGESTIONS

Never attempt to force your voice when hoarse.

Do not drink cold water when speaking. The sudden shock to the heated organs of speech will injure the voice.

Avoid pitching your voice too high—it will make it raspy. This is a common fault. When you find your voice in too high a range, lower it. Do not wait until you get to the platform to try this. Practice it in your daily conversation. Repeat the alphabet, beginning A on the lowest scale possible and going up a note on each succeeding letter, for the development of range. A wide range will give you facility in making numerous changes of pitch.

Do not form the habit of listening to your voice when speaking. You will need your brain to think of what you are saying—reserve your observation for private practice.

> **POINTS TO REMEMBER**
>
> 1. Follow the fundamental principles for a good voice—ease, openness, forwardness.
> 2. Practice voice exercises on a daily basis.
> 3. To get your voice heard, speak.

9

THE SIN OF MONOTONY

Our English has changed with the years so that many words now connote more than they did originally. This is true of the word monotonous. From 'having but one tone', it has come to mean more broadly, 'lack of variation'.

The monotonous speaker not only drones along in the same volume and pitch of tone but uses always the same emphasis, the same speed, the same thoughts—or dispenses with thought altogether.

Emerson says, 'The virtue of art lies in detachment, in sequestering one object from the embarrassing variety.' That is just what the monotonous speaker fails to do—he does not detach one thought or phrase from another, they are all expressed in the same manner.

To tell you that your speech is monotonous may mean very little to you, so let us look at the nature—and the curse—of monotony in other spheres of life, then we shall appreciate more fully how it will blight an otherwise good speech.

If the Victrola in the adjoining apartment plays just three songs over and over again, it is pretty safe to assume that your neighbour has no other records. If a speaker uses only a few of his powers, it points very plainly to the fact that the rest of his powers are not developed. Monotony reveals our limitations.

In its effect on its victim, monotony is actually deadly—it will drive the bloom from the cheek and the lustre from the eye as quickly as sin, and often leads to viciousness.

So, this thing that shortens life, and is used as the most cruel of punishments in our prisons, is the thing that will destroy all the life and force of a speech. Avoid it as you would shun a deadly dull bore. Monotony is poverty, whether in speech or in life. Strive to increase the variety of your speech as the businessman labours to augment his wealth.

Bird-songs, forest glens and mountains are not monotonous—it is the long rows of brown-stone fronts and the miles of paved streets that are so terribly same. Nature in her wealth gives us endless variety; man with his limitations is often monotonous. Get back to nature in your methods of speech-making.

The power of variety lies in its pleasure-giving quality. The great truths of the world have often been couched in fascinating stories—*Les Miserables*, for instance. If you wish to teach or influence men, you must please them, first or last. Strike the same note on the piano over and over again. This will give you some idea of the displeasing, jarring effect monotony has on the ear. The dictionary defines 'monotonous' as being synonymous with 'wearisome'. That is putting it mildly. It is maddening. The department-store prince does not disgust the public by playing only the one tune, 'Come Buy My Wares!' He gives recitals on a $125,000 organ, and the pleased people naturally slip into a buying mood.

HOW TO CONQUER MONOTONY

We obviate monotony in dress by replenishing our wardrobes. We avoid monotony in speech by multiplying our powers of speech. We multiply our powers of speech by increasing our tools.

The carpenter has special implements with which to construct the several parts of a building. The organist has certain keys and stops which he manipulates to produce his harmonies and effects. In like manner, the speaker has certain instruments and tools at his command by which he builds his argument, plays on the feelings and guides the beliefs of his audience. To give you a conception of these instruments, and practical help in learning to use them, are the purposes of the immediately following chapters.

It is useless to shoe a dead horse, and all the sound principles in Christendom will never make a live speech out of a dead one. So let it be understood that public speaking is not a matter of mastering a few dead rules; the most important law of public speech is the necessity for truth, force, feeling and life. Forget all else, but not this.

When you have mastered the mechanics of speech outlined in the next few chapters you will no longer be troubled with monotony. The complete knowledge of these principles and the ability to apply them will give you great variety in your powers of expression. But they cannot be mastered and applied by thinking or reading about them—you must practice, practice, PRACTICE. If no one else will listen to you, listen to yourself—you must always be your own best critic, and the severest one of all.

The technical principles that we lay down in the following chapters are not arbitrary creations of our own. They are all founded on the practices that good speakers and actors adopt—either naturally and unconsciously or under instruction—in getting their effects.

It is useless to warn the student that he must be natural. To be natural may be to be monotonous. The little strawberry up in the arctics with a few tiny seeds and an acid tang is a natural berry, but it is not to be compared with the improved variety that we enjoy here. The dwarfed oak on the rocky hillside is natural, but a poor thing compared with the beautiful tree found in the rich, moist bottom lands. Be natural—but improve your natural gifts until you have approached the ideal, for we must strive after idealized nature, in fruit, tree and speech.

POINTS TO REMEMBER

1. A monotonous speech is deadly.
2. Avoid monotony in speech by multiplying the powers of speech.
3. You must always be your own best critic, and the severest one of all.

10

MAKING IT HAPPEN

Look out the window. Notice how much change has occurred out there in just the past few years.

The post-war boom went bust. Competition became global. Consumers grew more sophisticated. Quality became an expectation. Whole new industries were born, and others were realigned. Some dried up and blew away. The idea of two military superpowers now seems like ancient history.

The Eastern Bloc fell apart. Europe is growing more unified by the day. The Third World countries are trying to elbow their way onto the economic stage. Most of the cushiness has gone out of modern capitalism—and with it the blessed stability that generations of business people had come to expect.

Did Dale Carnegie anticipate every one of these changes? Of course not. No one could have in a world changing so fast.

But Carnegie did something even more important. He left behind a timeless set of human-relations principles that are just as relevant today as they ever were. And as things turned out, they are uniquely suited to the current high-stress, fast-moving, uncertain world.

Look at things from the other person's perspective.
Offer genuine appreciation and praise.
Harness the mighty power of enthusiasm.

Respect the dignity of others.
Don't be overly critical.
Give people a good reputation to live up to.
Keep a sense of fun and balance in your life.

Three generations of students and business people have benefited from this essential wisdom. More people are benefiting every day.

The timelessness of Carnegie's principles should come as no surprise. They were never rooted in the realities of any particular moment, realities that are guaranteed to change and change. Carnegie tested his principles too long and hard for that. Fads would come and go over the years. Stocks would rise and fall. Technology would accelerate ahead. Political parties would win and lose. And the economic pendulum would swing like a hypnotist's watch—good times, bad times, good times, bad times...

But Carnegie's insights were solid. They merely needed to be applied. They were built around basic facts of human nature, so their essential truth never waned. They worked when the world was humming along. In this new era of constant change, they work just as well. Only now the need for Carnegie's principles—for anything that works—is greater than it's ever been.

So, apply these basic lessons and techniques. Make them part of your daily life. Use them with your friends, family, and colleagues. See what a difference they can make.

The Carnegie principles don't require an advanced degree in human psychology. They don't call for years of reflection and thought. All they take is practice, energy and a real desire to get along better in the world.

'The rules we have set down here are not mere theories or guesswork,' Dale Carnegie said about the principles he spent his life teaching to millions. 'They work like magic. Incredible as it sounds, I have seen the application of these principles literally revolutionize the lives of many people.'

So, take those words to heart, and find the leader in you.

POINTS TO REMEMBER

1. Look at things from the other person's perspective.
2. Offer genuine appreciation and praise.
3. Don't be overly critical.

11

FEELING AND ENTHUSIASM

If you are addressing a body of scientists on such a subject as the veins in a butterfly's wings or on road structure, naturally your theme will not arouse much feeling in either you or your audience. These are purely mental subjects. But if you want men to vote for a measure that will abolish child labour or if you would inspire them to take up arms for freedom, you must strike straight at their feelings. We lie on soft beds, sit near the radiator on a cold day, eat cherry pie and devote our attention to one of the opposite sex, not because we have reasoned out that it is the right thing to do, but because it feels right. No one but a dyspeptic chooses his diet from a chart. Our feelings dictate what we shall eat and generally how we shall act. Man is a feeling animal, hence the public speaker's ability to arouse men to action depends almost wholly on his ability to touch their emotions.

Negro mothers on the auction-block, seeing their children sold away from them into slavery, have flamed out some of America's most stirring speeches. True, the mother did not have any knowledge of the technique of speaking, but she had something greater than all technique, more effective than reason: feeling. The great speeches of the world have not been delivered on tariff reductions or post-office appropriations. The speeches that will live have been charged with emotional force. Prosperity and peace are poor developers of eloquence. When great wrongs are to be righted, when the public heart is flaming with passion, that is the occasion for memorable speaking. Patrick Henry made an immortal address, for in an epochal crisis he pleaded for liberty. He had roused himself to the point where he could honestly and passionately exclaim, 'Give me liberty or give me death.' His fame would have been different had he lived today and argued for the recall of judges.

THE POWER OF ENTHUSIASM

Political parties hire bands, and pay for applause—they argue that, for vote-getting, to stir up enthusiasm is more effective than reasoning. How far they are right depends on the hearers, but there can be no doubt about the contagious nature of enthusiasm. A watch manufacturer in New York tried out two series of watch advertisements; one argued the superior construction, workmanship, durability and guarantee offered with the watch; the other was headed, 'A Watch to be Proud of', and dwelt upon the pleasure and pride of ownership. The latter series sold twice as many as the former. A salesman for a locomotive works informed the writer that in selling railroad engines, emotional appeal was stronger than an argument based on mechanical excellence.

Illustrations without number might be cited to show that in all our actions we are emotional beings. The speaker who would speak efficiently must develop the power to arouse feeling.

Webster, great debater that he was, knew that the real secret of a speaker's power was an emotional one. He eloquently says of eloquence:

'Affected passion, intense expression, the pomp of declamation, all may aspire after it; they cannot reach it. It comes, if it come at all, like the outbreak of a fountain from the earth, or the bursting forth of volcanic fires, with spontaneous, original, native force.

The graces taught in the schools, the costly ornaments and studied contrivances of speech, shock and disgust men, when their own lives, and the fate of their wives, their children and their country hang on the decision of the hour. Then words have lost their power, rhetoric is in vain and all elaborate oratory contemptible. Even genius itself then feels rebuked and subdued, as in the presence of higher qualities. Then patriotism is eloquent, then self-devotion is eloquent. The clear conception outrunning the deductions of logic, the high purpose, the firm resolve, the dauntless spirit, speaking on the tongue, beaming from the eye, informing every feature and urging the whole man onward, right onward to his subject—this, this is eloquence; or rather, it is something greater and higher than all eloquence; it is action, noble, sublime, godlike action.'

When traveling through the Northwest some time ago, one of the present writers strolled up a village street after dinner and noticed a crowd listening to a 'faker' speaking at a corner from a goods-box. Remembering Emerson's advice about learning something from every man we meet, the observer stopped to listen to this speaker's appeal. He was selling a hair tonic, which he claimed to have discovered in Arizona. He removed his hat to show what this remedy had done for him, washed his face in it to demonstrate that it was as harmless as water, and enlarged on its merits in such an enthusiastic manner that the half-dollars poured in on him in a silver flood. When he had supplied the audience with hair tonic, he asked why a greater proportion of men than women were bald. No one knew. He explained that it was because women wore thinner-soled shoes, and so made a good electrical connection with mother earth, while men wore thick, dry-soled shoes that did not transmit the earth's electricity to the body. Men's hair, not having a proper amount of electrical food, died and fell out. Of course, he had a remedy—a little copper plate that should be nailed on the bottom of the shoe. He pictured in enthusiastic and vivid terms the desirability of escaping baldness—and paid tributes to his copper plates. Strange as it may seem when the story is told in cold print, the speaker's enthusiasm had swept his audience with him, and they crushed around his stand with outstretched quarters in their anxiety to be the possessors of these magical plates!

Emerson's suggestion had been well taken—the observer had seen again the wonderful, persuasive power of enthusiasm!

Enthusiasm sent millions crusading into the Holy Land to redeem it from the Saracens. Enthusiasm plunged Europe into a thirty years war over religion. Enthusiasm sent three small ships plying the unknown sea to the shores of a new world. When Napoleon's army were worn out and discouraged in their ascent of the Alps, the Little Corporal stopped them and ordered the bands to play the Marseillaise. Under its soul-stirring strains there were no Alps.

Listen! Emerson said, 'Nothing great was ever achieved without enthusiasm.' Carlyle declared that, 'Every great movement in the annals of history has been the triumph of enthusiasm.' It is as contagious as measles. Eloquence is half-inspiration. Sweep your audience with you in a pulsation of enthusiasm. Let yourself go. 'A man,' said Oliver Cromwell, 'never rises so high as when he knows not whither he is going.'

How are We to Acquire and Develop Enthusiasm?

It is not to be slipped on like a smoking-jacket. A book cannot furnish you with it. It is a growth—an effect. But an effect of what? Let us see.

Emerson wrote:

> A painter told me that nobody could draw a tree without in some sort becoming a tree; or draw a child by studying the outlines of his form merely—but, by watching for a time his motion and plays, the painter enters his nature and then can draw him at will in every attitude. So Roos, 'entered into the inmost nature of his sheep.' I knew a draughtsman employed in a public survey, who found that he could not sketch the rocks until their geological structure was first explained to him.

When Sarah Bernhardt plays a difficult role, she frequently will speak to no one from four o'clock in the afternoon until after the performance. From the hour of four she lives her character. Booth, it is reported, would not permit anyone to speak to him between the acts of his Shakesperean rôles, for he was Macbeth then—not Booth. Dante, exiled from his beloved Florence, condemned to death, lived in caves, half starved; then Dante wrote out his heart in *The Divine Comedy*. Bunyan entered into the spirit of his *Pilgrim's Progress* so thoroughly that he fell down on the floor of Bedford jail and wept for joy. Turner, who lived in a garret, arose before daybreak and walked over the hills nine miles to see the sun rise on the ocean, that he might catch the spirit of its wonderful beauty. Wendell Phillips' sentences were full of 'silent lightning' because he bore in his heart the sorrow of five million slaves.

There is only one way to get feeling into your speaking—and whatever else you forget, forget not this: You must actually

ENTER INTO the character you impersonate, the cause you advocate, the case you argue—enter into it so deeply that it clothes you, enthrals you, possesses you wholly. Then you are, in the true meaning of the word, in sympathy with your subject, for its feeling is your feeling, you 'feel with' it, and therefore your enthusiasm is both genuine and contagious. The Carpenter who spoke as 'never man spake', uttered words born out of a passion of love for humanity—he had entered into humanity, and thus become Man.

But we must not look upon the foregoing words as a facile prescription for decocting a feeling which may then be ladled out to a complacent audience in quantities to suit the need of the moment. Genuine feeling in a speech is bone and blood of the speech itself and not something that may be added to it or subtracted at will. In the ideal address theme, speaker and audience become one, fused by the emotion and thought of the hour.

THE NEED OF SYMPATHY FOR HUMANITY

It is impossible to lay too much stress on the necessity for the speaker's having a broad and deep tenderness for human nature. One of Victor Hugo's biographers attributes his power as an orator and writer to his wide sympathies and profound religious feelings. Recently we heard the editor of *Collier's Weekly* speak on short-story writing, and he so often emphasized the necessity for this broad love for humanity, this truly religious feeling, that he apologized twice for delivering a sermon. Few if any of the immortal speeches were ever delivered for a selfish or a narrow cause—they were born out of a passionate desire to help humanity; instances—Paul's address to the Athenians on Mars Hill, Lincoln's Gettysburg Address, The Sermon on the Mount,

Henry's address before the Virginia Convention of Delegates.

The seal and sign of greatness is a desire to serve others. Self-preservation is the first law of life, but self-abnegation is the first law of greatness—and of art. Selfishness is the fundamental cause of all sin, it is the thing that all great religions, all worthy philosophies, have struck at. Out of a heart of real sympathy and love come the speeches that move humanity.

Former United States Senator Albert J. Beveridge in an introduction to one of the volumes of *Modern Eloquence*, says:

> The profoundest feeling among the masses, the most influential element in their character, is the religious element. It is as instinctive and elemental as the law of self-preservation. It informs the whole intellect and personality of the people. And he who would greatly influence the people by uttering their unformed thoughts must have this great and unanalysable bond of sympathy with them.

When the men of Ulster armed themselves to oppose the passage of the Home Rule Act, one of the present writers assigned to a hundred men 'Home Rule' as the topic for an address to be prepared by each. Among this group were some brilliant speakers, several of them experienced lawyers and political campaigners. Some of their addresses showed a remarkable knowledge and grasp of the subject; others were clothed in the most attractive phrases. But a clerk, without a great deal of education and experience, arose and told how he spent his boyhood days in Ulster, how his mother while holding him on her lap had pictured to him Ulster's deeds of valour. He spoke of a picture in his uncle's home that showed the men of Ulster conquering a tyrant and marching on to victory. His voice quivered, and with a hand pointing upward he declared that if the men of Ulster went to war they would not go alone—a great God would go with them.

The speech thrilled and electrified the audience. It thrills yet as we recall it. The high-sounding phrases, the historical knowledge, the philosophical treatment of the other speakers largely failed to arouse any deep interest, while the genuine conviction and feeling of the modest clerk, speaking on a subject that lay deep in his heart, not only electrified his audience but also won their personal sympathy for the cause he advocated.

As Webster said, it is of no use to try to pretend to sympathy or feelings. It cannot be done successfully. 'Nature forever puts a premium on reality.' What is false is soon detected as such. The thoughts and feelings that create and mould the speech in the study must be born again when the speech is delivered from the platform. Do not let your words say one thing, and your voice and attitude another. There is no room here for half-hearted, nonchalant methods of delivery. Sincerity is the very soul of eloquence. Carlyle was right:

> No Mirabeau, Napoleon, Burns, Cromwell, no man adequate to do anything, but is first of all in right earnest about it; what I call a sincere man. I should say sincerity, a great, deep, genuine sincerity, is the first characteristic of all men in any way heroic. Not the sincerity that calls itself sincere; ah no, that is a very poor matter indeed; a shallow braggart, conscious sincerity, oftenest self-conceit mainly. The great man's sincerity is of the kind he cannot speak of—is not conscious of.

> **POINTS TO REMEMBER**
>
> 1. A great speech should be charged with emotional force.
> 2. Nothing great is ever achieved without enthusiasm.
> 3. Do not let your words say one thing, and your voice and attitude another.

12

A SURE WAY OF MAKING ENEMIES—AND HOW TO AVOID IT

When Theodore Roosevelt was in the White House, he confessed that if he could be right 75 per cent of the time, he would reach the highest measure of his expectation.

If that was the highest rating that one of the most distinguished men of the twentieth century could hope to obtain, what about you and me?

If you can be sure of being right only 55 per cent of the time, you can go down to Wall Street and make a million dollars a day. If you can't be sure of being right even 55 per cent of the time, why should you tell other people they are wrong?

You can tell people they are wrong by a look or an intonation or a gesture just as eloquently as you can in words—and if you tell them they are wrong, do you make them want to agree with you? Never! For you have struck a direct blow at their intelligence, judgment, pride and self-respect. That will make them want to strike back. But it will never make them want to change their minds. You may then hurl at them all the logic of a Plato or an Immanuel Kant, but you will not alter their opinions, for you have hurt their feelings.

Never begin by announcing, 'I am going to prove so-and-so

to you.' That's bad. That's tantamount to saying, 'I'm smarter than you are. I'm going to tell you a thing or two and make you change your mind.'

That is a challenge. It arouses opposition and makes the listener want to battle with you before you even start. It is difficult, under even the most benign conditions, to change people's minds. So why make it harder? Why handicap yourself?

Well, I can't hope to be any smarter than Socrates, so I have quit telling people they are wrong. And I find that it pays.

If a person makes a statement that you think is wrong—yes, even that you know is wrong—isn't it better to begin by saying, 'Well, now, look. I thought otherwise, but I may be wrong. I frequently am. And if I am wrong, I want to be put right. Let's examine the facts.'

There's magic, positive magic, in such phrases as, 'I may be wrong. I frequently am. Let's examine the facts.'

Nobody in the heavens above or on the earth will ever object to your saying, 'I may be wrong. Let's examine the facts.'

One of our class members who used this approach in dealing with customers was Harold Reinke, a Dodge dealer in Billings, Montana. He reported that because of the pressures of the automobile business, he was often hard-boiled and callous when dealing with customers complaints. This caused flared tempers, loss of business and general unpleasantness.

He told his class, 'Recognizing that this was getting me nowhere fast, I tried a new tack. I would say something like this, "Our dealership has made so many mistakes that I am frequently ashamed. We have erred in your case. Tell me about it."

'This approach becomes quite disarming, and by the time the customer releases his feelings, he is usually much more reasonable when it comes to settling the matter. In fact, several customers have thanked me for having such an understanding attitude. And two of them have even brought in friends to buy new cars. In this highly competitive market, we need more of this type of customer, and I believe that showing respect for all customers' opinions and treating them diplomatically and courteously will help beat the competition.'

You will never get into trouble by admitting that you may be wrong. That will stop all argument and inspire your opponent to be just as fair and open and broad-minded as you are. It will make him want to admit that he, too, may be wrong.

If you know positively that a person is wrong, and you bluntly tell him or her so, what happens? Let me illustrate. Mr S, a young New York attorney, once argued a rather important case before the United States Supreme Court *(Lustgarten v. Fleet Corporation 280 U.S. 320).* The case involved a considerable sum of money and an important question of law. During the argument, one of the Supreme Court justices said to him, 'The statute of limitations is six years, is it not?'

Mr S stopped, stared at the justice for a moment, and then said bluntly, 'Your Honour, there is no statute of limitations in admiralty.'

'A hush fell on the court,' said Mr S, as he related his experience to one of the author's classes, 'and the temperature in the room seemed to drop to zero. I was right. Justice was wrong. And I had told him so. But did that make him friendly? No. I still believe that I had the law on my side. And I know that I spoke better than I ever spoke before. But I didn't persuade. I made the enormous blunder of telling a very learned and famous man that he was wrong.'

Few people are logical. Most of us are prejudiced and biased. Most of us are blighted with preconceived notions, with jealousy, suspicion, fear, envy and pride. And most citizens don't want to change their minds about their religion or their haircut or communism or their favourite movie star.

Carl Rogers, the eminent psychologist, wrote in his book *On Becoming a Person:*

> I have found it of enormous value when I can permit myself to understand the other person. The way in which I have worded this statement may seem strange to you. Is it necessary to permit oneself to understand another? I think it is. Our first reaction to most of the statements [which we hear from other people] is an evaluation or judgment, rather than an understanding of it. When someone expresses some feeling, attitude or belief, our tendency is almost immediately to feel 'that's right,' or 'that's stupid,' 'that's abnormal,' 'that's unreasonable,' 'that's incorrect,' 'that's not nice.' Very rarely do we permit ourselves to understand precisely what the meaning of the statement is to the other person.

I once employed an interior decorator to make some draperies for my home. When the bill arrived, I was dismayed.

A few days later, a friend dropped in and looked at the draperies. The price was mentioned, and she exclaimed with a note of triumph, 'What? That's awful. I am afraid he put one over on you.'

True? Yes, she had told the truth, but few people like to listen to truths that reflect on their judgment. So, being human, I tried to defend myself. I pointed out that the best is eventually the cheapest, that one can't expect to get quality and artistic taste at bargain-basement prices and so on and on.

The next day another friend dropped in, admired the draperies, bubbled over with enthusiasm and expressed a wish that she could afford such exquisite creations for her home.

My reaction was totally different. 'Well, to tell the truth,' I said, 'I can't afford them myself. I paid too much. I'm sorry I ordered them.'

When we are wrong, we may admit it to ourselves. And if we are handled gently and tactfully, we may admit it to others and even take pride in our frankness and broad-mindedness. But not if someone else is trying to ram the unpalatable fact down our oesophagus.

Horace Greeley, the most famous editor in America during the time of the Civil War, disagreed violently with Lincoln's policies. He believed that he could drive Lincoln into agreeing with him by a campaign of argument, ridicule and abuse. He waged this bitter campaign month after month, year after year. In fact, he wrote a brutal, bitter, sarcastic and personal attack on President Lincoln the night Booth shot him.

But did all this bitterness make Lincoln agree with Greeley? Not at all. Ridicule and abuse never do.

DIPLOMACY WILL TAKE YOU PLACES

If you want some excellent suggestions about dealing with people and managing yourself and improving your personality, read Benjamin Franklin's autobiography—one of the most fascinating life stories ever written, one of the classics of American literature. Ben Franklin tells how he conquered the iniquitous habit of argument and transformed himself into one of the most able, suave and diplomatic men in American history.

One day, when Ben Franklin was a blundering youth, an old Quaker friend took him aside and lashed him with a few stinging truths, something like this:

> Ben, you are impossible. Your opinions have a slap in them for everyone who differs with you. They have become so offensive that nobody cares for them. Your friends find they enjoy themselves better when you are not around. You know so much that no man can tell you anything. Indeed, no man is going to try, for the effort would lead only to discomfort and hard work. So, you are not likely ever to know any more than you do now, which is very little.

One of the finest things I know about Ben Franklin is the way he accepted that smarting rebuke. He was big enough and wise enough to realize that it was true, to sense that he was headed for failure and social disaster. So, he made a right-about-face. He began immediately to change his insolent, opinionated ways.

'I made it a rule,' said Franklin, 'to forbear all direct contradiction to the sentiment of others, and all positive assertion of my own. I even forbade myself the use of every word or expression in the language that imported a fix'd opinion, such as "certainly," "undoubtedly," etc., and I adopted, instead of them, "I conceive," "I apprehend," or "I imagine" a thing to be so or so, or "it so appears to me at present." When another asserted something that I thought an error, I deny'd myself the pleasure of contradicting him abruptly, and of showing immediately some absurdity in his proposition: and in answering I began by observing that in certain cases or instances his opinion would be right, but in the present case there appear'd or seem'd to me some difference, etc. I soon found the advantage of this change in my manner; the conversations I engag'd in went on more pleasantly. The modest way in which I propos'd my opinions procur'd them a readier reception and less contradiction; I had less mortification when I was found to be in the wrong, and I more easily prevail'd with others to give up their mistakes and join with me when I happened to be in the right.

'And this mode, which I at first put on with some violence to natural inclination, became at length so easy, and so habitual to me, that perhaps for these fifty years past no one has ever heard a dogmatical expression escape me. And to this habit (after my character of integrity) I think it principally owing that I had earned so much weight with my fellow citizens when I proposed new institutions, or alterations in the old, and so much influence in public councils when I became a member; for I was but a bad speaker, never eloquent, subject to much hesitation in my choice of words, hardly correct in language, and yet I generally carried my points.'

How do Ben Franklin's methods work in business? Let's take two examples.

Katherine A. Allred of Kings Mountain, North Carolina, is an industrial engineering supervisor for a yarn-processing plant. She told one of our classes how she handled a sensitive problem before and after taking our training,

'Part of my responsibility,' she reported, 'deals with setting up and maintaining incentive systems and standards for our operators so they can make more money by producing more yarn. The system we were using had worked fine when we had only two or three different types of yarn, but recently we had expanded our inventory and capabilities to enable us to run more than twelve different varieties. The present system was no longer adequate to pay the operators fairly for the work being performed and give them an incentive to increase production. I had worked up a new system which would enable us to pay the operator by the class of yarn she was running at any one particular time. With my new system in hand, I entered the meeting determined to prove to the management that my system was the right approach. I told them in detail how they were wrong and showed where they were being unfair and how I had all the answers they needed. To say the least, I failed miserably! I had become so busy defending my position on the new system that I had left them no opening to graciously admit their problems on the old one. The issue was dead.

'After several sessions of this course, I realized all too well where I had made my mistakes. I called another meeting and this time I asked where they felt their problems were. We discussed each point, and I asked them their opinions on which was the best way to proceed. With a few low-keyed suggestions, at proper intervals, I let them develop my system themselves. At the end of the meeting when I actually presented my system, they enthusiastically accepted it.

'I am convinced now that nothing good is accomplished and a lot of damage can be done if you tell a person straight out that he or she is wrong. You only succeed in stripping that person of self-dignity and making yourself an unwelcome part of any discussion.'

Let's take another example—and remember these cases I am citing are typical of the experiences of thousands of other people. R. V. Crowley was a salesman for a lumber company in New York. Crowley admitted that he had been telling hard-boiled lumber inspectors for years that they were wrong. And he had won the arguments too. But it hadn't done any good. 'For these lumber inspectors,' said Mr. Crowley, 'are like baseball umpires. Once they make a decision, they never change it.'

Mr. Crowley saw that his firm was losing thousands of dollars through the arguments he won. So, while taking my course, he resolved to change tactics and abandon arguments. With what results? Here is the story as he told it to the fellow members of his class,

'One morning the phone rang in my office. A hot and bothered person at the other end proceeded to inform me that a car of lumber we had shipped into his plant was entirely unsatisfactory. His firm had stopped unloading and requested that we make immediate arrangements to remove the stock from their yard. After about one-fourth of the car had been unloaded, their lumber inspector reported that the lumber was running 55 per cent below grade. Under the circumstances, they refused to accept it.

'I immediately started for his plant and on the way turned over in my mind the best way to handle the situation. Ordinarily, under such circumstances, I should have quoted grading rules and tried, as a result of my own experience and knowledge as a lumber inspector, to convince the other inspector that the lumber was actually up to grade, and that he was misinterpreting the rules in his inspection. However, I thought I would apply the principles learned in this training.

'When I arrived at the plant, I found the purchasing agent and the lumber inspector in a wicked humour, both set for an argument and a fight. We walked out to the car that was being unloaded, and I requested that they continue to unload so that I could see how things were going. I asked the inspector to go right ahead and lay out the rejects, as he had been doing, and to put the good pieces in another pile.

'After watching him for a while it began to dawn on me that his inspection actually was much too strict and that he was misinterpreting the rules. This particular lumber was white pine, and I knew the inspector was thoroughly schooled in hard woods but not a competent, experienced inspector on white pine. White pine happened to be my own strong suit, but did I offer any objection to the way he was grading the lumber? None whatever. I kept on watching and gradually began to ask questions as to why certain pieces were not satisfactory. I didn't for one instant insinuate that the inspector was wrong. I emphasized that my only reason for asking was in order that we could give his firm exactly what they wanted in future shipments.

'By asking questions in a very friendly, cooperative spirit, and insisting continually that they were right in laying out boards not satisfactory to their purpose, I got him warmed up, and the strained relations between us began to thaw and melt away. An occasional carefully put remark on my part gave birth to the idea in his mind that possibly some of these rejected pieces were actually within the grade that they had bought, and that their requirements demanded a more expensive grade. I was very careful, however, not to let him think I was making an issue of this point.

'Gradually his whole attitude changed. He finally admitted to me that he was not experienced on white pine and began to ask me questions about each piece as it came out of the car. I would explain why such a piece came within the grade specified, but kept on insisting that we did not want him to take it if it was unsuitable for their purpose. He finally got to the point where he felt guilty every time he put a piece in the rejected pile. And at last he saw that the mistake was on their part for not having specified as good a grade as they needed.

'The ultimate outcome was that he went through the entire carload again after I left, accepted the whole lot, and we received a check in full.

'In that one instance alone, a little tact, and the determination to refrain from telling the other man he was wrong, saved my company a substantial amount of cash, and it would be hard to place a money value on the good will that was saved.'

Martin Luther King, Jr., was asked how, as a pacifist, he

could be an admirer of Air Force General Daniel 'Chappie' James, then the nation's highest-ranking black officer. Dr. King replied, 'I judge people by their own principles—not by my own.'

In a similar way, General Robert E. Lee once spoke to the president of the Confederacy, Jefferson Davis in the most glowing terms about a certain officer under his command. Another officer was astonished. 'General,' he said, 'do you not know that the man of whom you speak so highly is one of your bitterest enemies who misses no opportunity to malign you?' 'Yes,' replied General Lee, 'but the president asked my opinion of him; he did not ask for his opinion of me.'

By the way, I am not revealing anything new in this chapter. Two thousand years ago, Jesus said, 'Agree with thine adversary quickly.'

And twenty-two hundred years before Christ was born, Pharaoh Akhtoi of Egypt gave his son some shrewd advice—advice that is sorely needed today. 'Be diplomatic,' counselled the pharaoh. 'It will help you gain your point.'

In other words, don't argue with your customer or your spouse or your adversary. Don't tell them they are wrong, don't get them stirred up. Use a little diplomacy.

POINTS TO REMEMBER

1. Quit telling people they are wrong.
2. Admit you are at fault and you'll never get into trouble.
3. Be Switzerland.

13

HANDLING MISTAKES, COMPLAINTS, AND CRITICISM

Barend Hendrik Strydom was a vicious, cold-blooded killer. Strydom, a white South African, was angry about the progress blacks were finally making in that land of racial apartheid. So, one day in 1988 he decided to do something about it. He sprayed a crowd of black protesters with machine-gun fire, hitting nine men and women, leaving eight of them dead.

He was tried, convicted and sent off to death row. But even then, he didn't seem to think he had done anything to be criticized about. 'To have remorse, one must have done something wrong,' he said. 'I have done nothing wrong.'

When a legal technicality got Strydom's sentence changed from the death penalty to life in jail, he still didn't seem to understand the public outcry that his crime had caused. 'I'll kill again,' he said. 'I have done nothing wrong.'

If such a brutal killer doesn't blame himself for his horrific crime, what about the people most of us come into contact with every day? Do you think they're eager to admit mistakes or be criticized?

There are two fundamental facts about mistakes. Number

one, we all make 'em. Number two, we're more than happy to point them out in others, but boy, how we hate it when someone points out one of ours!

Noel Coward was as thin-skinned about criticism as anyone, but at least he had a sense of humour. 'I love criticism just so long as it's unqualified praise,' the English playwright said.

No one—absolutely no one—likes to be on the receiving end of a complaint, a criticism or a rotten review. We all bristle when the finger of responsibility is pointed at us. This is easy enough to understand. Nothing stings the ego like being told we've made a bad decision or supervised a failed project or performed below expectations. It's even more difficult when the criticism turns out to be correct.

But mistakes get made. Arguments arise. Complaints, both legitimate and exaggerated, get lodged day after day. Customers are unhappy. Nobody is on target all the time.

So how do you handle the knowledge that nobody's perfect but criticism is hard to swallow? With a little practice and the help of a few time-tested human-relations techniques. Let's not deny the obvious. It's not always easy keeping both balls in the air. But it's not impossible either. After a while this particular juggling act can be mastered by almost anyone.

The first step is to create an environment where people are open to receiving advice or constructive criticism. Spread the word again and again that mistakes are a natural part of life.

One sure way to get this message across is to *admit your own mistakes*. 'Setting the example is very important. You can't expect from others what you're not willing to expect from yourself,' says Fred Sievert of New York Life Insurance Company. Shortly after he arrived at the company, Sievert had an opportunity to put his ego where his mouth was.

Sievert explains, 'I did something here that kind of astounded people. I was off in France at an executive management school, and we had some critical data that had to be submitted. It was our five-year plan, and there was a misunderstanding because it was my first time through this. Just before I left, we submitted the numbers. I was gone for two weeks. Of course, I was in touch via voicemail and fax. But we submitted the numbers, and there was a major crisis that occurred here. The problem was that I misunderstood the timing of this submission. I thought the initial submission was meant to be our first run of the numbers. I thought we then had plenty of time to analyse and talk about management actions that could be taken to improve the numbers. As it turns out, I didn't understand the process, and the first set of numbers that were given to the executive management committee and the chairman were viewed as our version of the plan. I didn't know that.

'Well, it created a tremendous problem because the numbers weren't good. There were inconsistencies. There were management actions we hadn't reflected, and I was off in France sending these voicemails back and forth, not really understanding what had happened but knowing there was a crisis. I volunteered to come back, but my boss said, "No, we got it handled."

'When I got back I realized what had happened. After talking to various people—I know these people were shocked—I said at a meeting, "This is my fault. It's a communication issue. It wasn't a matter of not understanding the numbers. It was a matter of communication, and it was entirely my fault."

'While I was gone, people were pointing the finger at each other. My staff was saying, "Why didn't you guys tell us this was our last shot at this?" And the other people were saying, "You should have understood this was the last shot." Okay, everybody's pointing the finger, and I came in and stood up and said, "This is entirely my fault. I take full responsibility for it. It's a communication problem. It won't happen again." And you know that statement put an end to all the finger pointing. Several people in the room said, "No, no, no, it wasn't your fault. You know it was a combination of people."'

Readily admitting fault—it's one of the best ways anyone has ever invented for shifting momentum when blame is being distributed. Be the first to admit mistakes. Everyone else will rush to reassure you, 'No, it's not so bad; no, it doesn't really matter; no, *they* probably were to blame; no, it all turned out fine in the end.'

Take the opposite tack—blame other people for something—and just as quickly they'll start to contradict you, and they'll defend the correctness of their actions. Funny, isn't it, how human psychology works?

This is true for all relationships—inside a company, a family or a group of friends. And it's true in customer or vendor relationships as well.

When a customer is unhappy about a product or the service that's been provided, a quick and forceful admission of error can often work wonders. That's what John Imlay discovered when he inadvertently offended an important customer. 'Back in 1987,' recalls Imlay, chairman of Dun & Bradstreet Software, 'I had to give a speech on the west coast of the United States to a group of chief information officers, I guess about a thousand of them. It was out at the Laguna Beach Hotel. To open it, I was talking about what's in and what out.

'"Noriega's out, democracy's in." Things like that. And the last one was, "Teenage Mutant Ninja Turtles are in, Ken and Barbie are out."

Everybody laughed except one fellow, one of my key customers. He was the head of Mattel.

'So, before I returned to the office, I received a letter. The letter said, "I enjoyed your speech, but you made one statement that I want you to retract forever." He went on in a blistering way, finally summing up by saying the sales of Barbie were more than the revenues of all my companies combined. So, I wrote him a letter apologizing, and I wrote Barbie a letter. He didn't think that was funny, either.'

Did Imlay give up there? Absolutely not. 'For years,' he said, 'I took his letter and put it into a slot, and every speech I gave I reminded the audience how you have to be sensitive to the customer's issues, and customers absolutely love the slot. I showed the letter, and how I had gotten it.

'One day I spoke at the Waldorf-Astoria in New York, and the president of Mattel was there. I gave this speech not knowing he was in the audience. As I spoke, someone passed me a note saying that the president of Mattel was there. I had him stand up, and he came up and shook my hand. Then he dropped me a note afterward saying all is forgiven, and he's been a happy customer ever since.'

The lesson here: admit your mistakes before anyone else has a chance to point them out. Laugh about them if you can. Never seek to minimize the impact they've had. 'A leader has to be responsible and accountable for his or her own mistakes,' says Fred Sievert. 'The worst thing you can do is to begin to point your finger at everybody else. You've got to take responsibility.' Or as Andrés Navarro says, 'If an organization is able to admit mistakes, it's encouraging creativity and encouraging people to take risks.'

DISCARD YOUR FIRST IDEA, ALWAYS

The second step for handling mistakes or problems: *think twice before you criticize or assign blame.* If the person who made the mistake already knows how it happened, why it happened and what needs to be done so it won't happen again, then nothing at all needs to be said. There's no point in making people feel worse than they already do.

Motivated employees *want* to perform well. G. Curt Jones, senior quality executive at the Federal Quality Institute, says, 'People don't come to work to mess up. They want to feel needed. They want to be committed.' Business leaders who understand that understand how destructive most criticism is.

The point is avoiding the blame game, and Ray Stata, the chairman of Analog Devices, Inc., knows all about it. 'The instinctive question when something goes wrong is, "Who's to blame?"' Stata observes. 'It's the way the human mind is wired. You want to find somebody to blame and talk about their mistakes.'

Stata is trying to rid Analog Devices of all unnecessary blame. 'One of the things that I'm cutting out is preaching in the organization,' he said. 'We all tend to do it. You know, commiserate, blame, when things aren't going right. Now, I think one of the little tricks is for me to set the example of converting complaints into requests and suggestions.'

You have to ask yourself, 'What am I trying to accomplish here?' Says Stata, "At the end of the day, what you want to do is create effective action that makes the place better. And talking about who was wrong or what's to blame is not it.' The real goal is to improve the situation.

Jack Gallagher had a major problem on his hands. Gallagher is the president of North Shore University Hospital, a 755-bed institution affiliated with Cornell University Medical College. As North Shore grew over the years, the hospital was stuck with the same kitchen that had been adequate in the days of 169 beds.

When the time finally came to build a new kitchen, Gallagher asked an associate to oversee the job. He gave the man two pieces of advice: hire a parking consultant and hire a dietary consultant.

'I couldn't follow the project every day,' Gallagher recalls. 'And for some reason, he didn't use the parking consultant. He didn't use the dietary consultant. So, we got trapped between the opening of the new kitchen and the closing of the old.'

By the time Gallagher discovered this, construction was already under way and millions had already been spent. It was much too late to change the plans. But no one was happy with the results. The new kitchen was too small, the quality of the food was slipping, and the hospital's reputation was suffering as a result.

Gallagher could have fired the associate. He could have criticized the man in public. But what good would that have done? How would a public scolding have improved the lamb chops or the baked chicken? Would it have made the string beans stay hot?

'You don't want to point a finger and assign blame,' Gallagher says. 'What we had to do was fix the system. We had to make it better. We had to step back and say, "How can we improve the situation?" Blame wouldn't have gotten us any closer to that.'

Criticism or blame spreading almost always causes people to duck and hide. People who have been on the receiving end of harsh criticism are far less likely to take risks, to be creative, to go out on a limb of any kind. Instantly the organization has lost an important part of that employee's potential.

This concept has found its way into the whole employee-review process at Mary Kay Corporation. The goal is improvement, not judgment. 'We don't call that a performance appraisal, we call it performance development,' said Mary Kay Vice Chairman Richard Bartlett. Why's that? 'I don't want to sit there and be judgmental,' Bartlett says. 'I want to know how I can help you be better. The big thing is we're sitting down and discussing your career at Mary Kay. How do you need to develop to be whatever it is you want to be in the future? From your viewpoint.' Now that's the kind of corporate attitude that invites and encourages employee innovation.

'The people who accept criticism the best are the people who are genuinely interested in self-improvement,' according to David Luther, the Corning quality chief. 'Sometimes the easiest people to correct are those who are at the top of the league. They're the people who are going for the extra five percent and welcome constructive criticism. One of the advantages of the Japanese is their notion of treasuring errors. They consider the discovery of a mistake or error as a treasure because it's a key toward further improvement.'

We all agree: almost no one likes to receive it, and far too many people like to give it. Blaming someone rarely improves the situation.

There are exceptions, of course. Sometimes people do need to be criticized constructively. If the need is urgent enough, if the danger is severe enough and if the mistake is made often enough, then something needs to be said. If after thoughtful consideration, you do decide you have to discuss a situation, *criticize respectfully*.

That's step number three. Walk softly and leave the big stick at home. Restrain yourself, follow a few basic techniques, and you'll ensure that your words are met by open ears.

Create a receptive environment for what you have to say. While people don't ever like to hear negative things about themselves, they'll be more receptive if you focus on the things they do right as well as the things they do wrong.

'The process of criticism should begin with praise and honest appreciation,' Dale Carnegie said. Mary Poppins had much the same thing in mind when she sang, 'A spoonful of sugar helps the medicine go down.'

Andrés Navarro at SONDA, S.A., has found a way to institutionalize a kinder, gentler approach to criticism. In his company there is now a three-for-one rule. Navarro explains, 'We try to criticize as little as we can. We have a rule. If you get into this company and you find someone whom you don't like and you think doesn't do his work the way he should, don't say anything. Write it down on a piece of paper. Once you discover three good things about the person whom you're talking about—or about a policy or a rule or a habit that we have—then you have the right to criticize one.' That's a great technique.

Another one is using encouragement. Make the faults seem easy to correct. This is the same principle that is practiced by New York Life's Fred Sievert. He calls it his 'sandwich technique' for giving criticism. 'I start by talking about the positive things that the employee has accomplished,' Sievert says. 'Then in the middle we talk about the areas for development and improvement. Finally, we close with a discussion of how valuable the person is to New York Life. It always works. I had a boss once who did that with me, and I used to walk out of the room scratching my head, saying, "Gee, I really feel good about getting reprimanded."'

DON'T STOOP LOW

Equally important is knowing what to avoid. Never argue, demean or shout at someone. If you're arguing with someone, you've already lost. You've lost control of yourself, you've lost your perspective and, most significantly, you've lost sight of your goal: to communicate, to persuade, to motivate.

As Dale Carnegie said, 'There is only one way under high heaven to get the best of an argument—and that is to avoid it. Avoid it as you would avoid rattlesnakes and earthquakes. Nine times out of ten, an argument ends with each of the contestants being more firmly convinced than ever that he is absolutely right.'

Let the person save face at all costs. This may mean hanging back in a discussion, calling attention to the person's mistakes indirectly or asking questions instead of giving orders. Or it may mean saving some criticism for another day. However, you choose to do it, the goal is the same: be gentle, underplay, don't attack. Even if someone doesn't agree entirely with your point of view, with enough finesse you may still get that person to see some merit in your position. But if you come on too strong, if you use words like *right* and *wrong*, *smart* and *stupid*, you'll never persuade anyone of anything.

'We do get complaints,' Wolfgang Schmitt of Rubbermaid says. 'About half of those complaints come about as the result of a consumer's buying a product, thinking it's ours, but it's a competitor's product. So, the consumer writes to us. Our policy is simply to write a personal letter and say, "We can understand how you made the mistake because we have these competitors who copy our products. You made an honest mistake, but we would like for you to see directly the difference in value. So try one of ours for free."

'We send them our replacement product for whatever it is they complained about. And we think that's a wonderful way to communicate very credibly the story of Rubbermaid value.'

Gentle persuasion always works better than screaming and

finger pointing. When you need to remind yourself of this, recall the old Aesop fable about the contest between the wind and the sun. The wind and the sun argued one day over which was stronger. The wind proposed a contest and, seeing an old man walking down the street, set the terms of the bet: whoever could get the man to remove his coat first would win. The sun agreed and the wind went first. The wind blew, harder and harder, until the gusts almost reached tornado force. But the harder the wind blew, the tighter the man clutched his coat.

When the wind gave up, the sun had its chance. The sun shone on the man gently, becoming warmer and warmer until the man, wiping his brow, took off his coat. The sun told the wind its secret: gentleness and friendliness are stronger than force and fury. The same rule applies to customers, to employees, to co-workers, to friends.

Dale Carnegie had a student in one of his classes who was a tax consultant. The student, Frederick Parsons, had a disagreement with an IRS agent about how to classify a nine-thousand-dollar debt. Parsons was arguing that the money was a bad debt that had not been paid and therefore wasn't taxable income. The agent was equally adamant that it was taxable.

Parsons was getting nowhere. So he decided to try a different approach, 'I decided to avoid the argument, change the subject, and give him appreciation. I said, "I suppose this is a very petty matter in comparison with the really important and difficult decisions you're required to make. I've made a study of taxation myself, but I've had to get my knowledge from books. You are getting yours from the firing line of experience. I sometimes wish I had a job like yours. It would teach me a lot." I meant every word.'

The result? 'The inspector straightened up in his chair, leaned back and talked for a long time about his work, telling me of the clever frauds he had uncovered. His tone gradually became friendly, and soon he was telling me about his children. As he left, he advised me that he would consider my problem further and give me his decision in a few days. He called at my office three days later and informed me that he had decided to leave the tax return exactly as it had been filed.'

What changed the tax inspector's mind? 'The tax inspector was demonstrating one of the most common of human frailties,' Carnegie wrote. 'He wanted a feeling of importance.'

As long as Mr. Parsons argued with him, he got his feeling of importance by loudly asserting his authority. But as soon as his importance was admitted and the argument stopped and he was permitted to expand his ego, he became a sympathetic and kindly human being.

BE QUICK TO ADMIT MISTAKES AND SLOW TO CRITICIZE. ABOVE ALL, BE CONSTRUCTIVE.

POINTS TO REMEMBER

1. The two fundamental facts about mistakes.
2. No one—absolutely no one—likes to be on the receiving end of a complaint.
3. Admit to your own mistakes.

14

THE MOVIES DO IT. TV DOES IT. WHY DON'T YOU DO IT?

Many years ago, the Philadelphia *Evening Bulletin* was being maligned by a dangerous whispering campaign. A malicious rumour was being circulated. Advertisers were being told that the newspaper was no longer attractive to readers because it carried too much advertising and too little news. Immediate action was necessary. The gossip had to be squelched.

But how?

This is the way it was done.

The *Bulletin* clipped from its regular edition all reading matter of all kinds on one average day, classified it and published it as a book. The book was called *One Day*. It contained 307 pages—as many as a hard-covered book; yet the *Bulletin* had printed all this news and feature material on one day and sold it, not for several dollars, but for a few cents.

The printing of that book dramatized the fact that the *Bulletin* carried an enormous amount of interesting reading matter. It conveyed the facts more vividly, more interestingly, more impressively, than pages of figures and mere talk could have done.

This is the day of dramatization. Merely stating a truth

isn't enough. The truth has to be made vivid, interesting and dramatic. You have to use showmanship. The movies do it. Television does it. And you will have to do it if you want attention.

Experts in window display know the power of dramatization. For example, the manufacturers of a new rat poison gave dealers a window display that included two live rats. The week the rats were shown, sales zoomed to five times their normal rate.

Television commercials abound with examples of the use of dramatic techniques in selling products. Sit down one evening in front of your television set and analyse what the advertisers do in each of their presentations. You will note how an antacid medicine changes the colour of the acid in a test tube while its competitor doesn't, how one brand of soap or detergent gets a greasy shirt clean when the other brand leaves it grey. You'll see a car manoeuvre around a series of turns and curves—far better than just being told about it. Happy faces will show contentment with a variety of products. All of these dramatize for the viewer the advantages offered by whatever is being sold—and they do get people to buy them.

You can dramatize your ideas in business or in any other aspect of your life. It's easy. Jim Yeamans, who sells for the NCR company (National Cash Register) in Richmond, Virginia, told how he made a sale by dramatic demonstration.

'Last week I called on a neighbourhood grocer and saw that the cash registers he was using at his checkout counters were very old-fashioned. I approached the owner and told him, 'You are literally throwing away pennies every time a customer goes through your line.' With that I threw a handful of pennies on the floor. He quickly became more attentive. The mere words should have been of interest to him, but the sound of pennies hitting the floor really stopped him. I was able to get an order from him to replace all of his old machines.'

It works in home life as well. When the old-time lover proposed to his sweetheart, did he just use words of love? No! He went down on his knees. That really showed he meant what he said. We don't propose on our knees any more, but many suitors still set up a romantic atmosphere before they pop the question.

Dramatizing what you want works with children as well. Joe B. Fant Jr., of Birmingham, Alabama, was having difficulty getting his five-year-old boy and three-year-old daughter to pick up their toys, so he invented a 'train'. Joey was the engineer (Captain Casey Jones) on his tricycle. Janet's wagon was attached, and in the evening, she loaded all the 'coal' on the caboose (her wagon) and then jumped in while her brother drove her around the room. In this way the room was cleaned up—without lectures, arguments or threats.

Mary Catherine Wolf of Mishawaka, Indiana, was having some problems at work and decided that she had to discuss them with the boss. On Monday morning she requested an appointment with him but was told he was very busy and she should arrange with his secretary for an appointment later in the week. The secretary indicated that his schedule was very tight, but she would try to fit her in.

Ms Wolf described what happened:

'I did not get a reply from her all week long. Whenever I questioned her, she would give me a reason why the boss could not see me. Friday morning came and I had heard nothing definite. I really wanted to see him and discuss my problems before the weekend, so I asked myself how I could get him to see me.

'What I finally did was this. I wrote him a formal letter. I indicated in the letter that I fully understood how extremely busy he was all week, but it was important that I speak with him. I enclosed a form letter and a self-addressed envelope and asked him to please fill it out or ask his secretary to do it and return it to me. The form letter read as follows:

Ms Wolf—I will be able to see you on—at—A.M./P.M. I will give you—minutes of my time.

'I put this letter in his in-basket at 11 am. At 2 pm I checked my mailbox. There was my self-addressed envelope. He had answered my form letter himself and indicated he could see me that afternoon and could give me ten minutes of his time. I met with him, and we talked for over an hour and resolved my problems.

'If I had not dramatized to him the fact that I really wanted to see him. I would probably be still waiting for an appointment.'

James B. Boynton had to present a lengthy market report. His firm had just finished an exhaustive study for a leading brand of cold cream. Data were needed immediately about the competition in this market; the prospective customer was one of the biggest—and most formidable—men in the advertising business.

And his first approach failed almost before he began.

'The first time I went in,' Mr Boynton explains, 'I found myself side-tracked into a futile discussion of the methods used in the investigation. He argued and I argued. He told me I was wrong, and I tried to prove that I was right.

'I finally won my point, to my own satisfaction—but my time was up, the interview was over, and I still hadn't produced results.

'The second time, I didn't bother with tabulations of figures and data. I went to see this man; I dramatized my facts.

'As I entered his office, he was busy on the phone. While

he finished his conversation, I opened a suitcase and dumped thirty-two jars of cold cream on top of his desk—all products he knew—all competitors of his cream.

'On each jar, I had a tag itemising the results of the trade investigation. And each tag told its story briefly, dramatically.

'What happened?

'There was no longer an argument. Here was something new, something different. He picked up first one then another of the jars of cold cream and read the information on the tag. A friendly conversation developed. He asked additional questions. He was intensely interested. He had originally given me only ten minutes to present my facts, but ten minutes passed, twenty minutes, forty minutes and at the end of an hour we were still talking.

'I was presenting the same facts this time that I had presented previously. But this time I was using dramatization, showmanship—and what a difference it made.'

POINTS TO REMEMBER

1. Know the power of dramatization.
2. People of all age groups are attracted to dramatics.
3. Enthusiasm reforms a good idea into a great one.

15

MAKING PEOPLE GLAD WHILE DOING WHAT YOU WANT

Back in 1915, America was aghast. For more than a year, the nations of Europe had been slaughtering one another on a scale never before dreamed of in all the bloody annals of mankind. Could peace be brought about? No one knew. But Woodrow Wilson was determined to try. He would send a personal representative, a peace emissary, to counsel with the warlords of Europe.

William Jennings Bryan, secretary of state, Bryan, the peace advocate, longed to go. He saw a chance to perform a great service and make his name immortal. But Wilson appointed another man, his intimate friend and adviser Colonel Edward M. House; and it was House's thorny task to break the unwelcome news to Bryan without giving him offence.

'Bryan was distinctly disappointed when he heard I was to go to Europe as the peace emissary,' Colonel House records in his diary. 'He said he had planned to do this himself...

'I replied that the President thought it would be unwise for anyone to do this officially, and *that his going would attract a great deal of attention* and people would wonder why he was there...'

You see the intimation? House practically told Bryan that he was *too important* for the job—and Bryan was satisfied.

Colonel House, adroit, experienced in the ways of the world, was following one of the important rules of human relations: *always make the other person happy about doing the thing you suggest.*

Woodrow Wilson followed that policy even when inviting William Gibbs McAdoo to become a member of his cabinet. That was the highest honour he could confer upon anyone, and yet Wilson extended the invitation in such a way as to make McAdoo feel doubly important. Here is the story in McAdoo's own words, 'He [Wilson] said that he was making up his cabinet and that he would be very glad if I would accept a place in it as Secretary of the Treasury. He had a delightful way of putting things; he created the impression that by accepting this great honour I would be doing him a favour.'

Unfortunately, Wilson didn't always employ such tact. If he had, history might have been different. For example, Wilson didn't make the Senate and the Republican Party happy by entering the United States in the League of Nations. Wilson refused to take such prominent Republican leaders as Elihu Root or Charles Evans Hughes or Henry Cabot Lodge to the peace conference with him. Instead, he took along unknown men from his own party. He snubbed the Republicans, refused to let them feel that the League was their idea as well as his, refused to let them have a finger in the pie; and, as a result of this crude handling of human relations, wrecked his own career, ruined his health, shortened his life, caused America to stay out of the League and altered the history of the world.

Statesmen and diplomats aren't the only ones who use this make-a-person-happy-to-do-things-you-want-them-to-do-approach. Dale O. Ferrier of Fort Wayne, Indiana, told how he encouraged one of his young children to willingly do the chore he was assigned.

'One of Jeff's chores was to pick up pears from under the pear tree so the person who was mowing underneath wouldn't have to stop to pick them up. He didn't like this chore, and frequently it was either not done at all or it was done so poorly that the mower had to stop and pick up several pears that he had missed. Rather than have an eyeball-to-eyeball confrontation about it, one day I said to him, "Jeff, I'll make a deal with you. For every bushel basket full of pears you pick up, I'll pay you one dollar. But after you are finished, for every pear I find left in the yard, I'll take away a dollar. How does that sound?" As you would expect, he not only picked up all of the pears, but I had to keep an eye on him to see that he didn't pull a few off the trees to fill up some of the baskets.'

I knew a man who had to refuse many invitations to speak, invitations extended by friends, invitations coming from people to whom he was obligated; and yet he did it so adroitly that the other person was at least contented with his refusal. How did he do it? Not by merely talking about the fact that he was too busy and too-this and too-that. No, after expressing his appreciation of the invitation and regretting his inability to accept it, he suggested a substitute speaker. In other words, he didn't give the other person any time to feel unhappy about the refusal. He immediately changed the other person's thoughts to some other speaker who could accept the invitation.

Gunter Schmidt, who took our course in West Germany, told of an employee in the food store he managed who was negligent about putting the proper price tags on the shelves where the items were displayed. This caused confusion and customer complaints. Reminders, admonitions, confrontations with her about this did not do much good. Finally, Mr Schmidt called her into his office and told her he was appointing her Supervisor of Price Tag Posting for the entire store and she would be responsible for keeping all of the shelves properly tagged. This new responsibility and title changed her attitude completely, and she fulfilled her duties satisfactorily from then on.

Childish? Perhaps. But that is what they said to Napoleon when he created the Legion of Honour and distributed 15,000 crosses to his soldiers and made eighteen of his generals 'Marshals of France' and called his troops the 'Grand Army'. Napoleon was criticised for giving 'toys' to war-hardened veterans, and Napoleon replied, 'Men are ruled by toys.'

This technique of giving titles and authority worked for Napoleon and it will work for you. For example, a friend of mine, Mrs Ernest Gent of Scarsdale, New York, was troubled by boys running across and destroying her lawn. She tried coaxing. Neither worked. Then she tried giving the worst sinner in the gang a title and a feeling of authority. She made him her 'detective' and put him in charge of keeping all trespassers off her lawn. That solved her problem. Her 'detective' built a bonfire in the backyard, heated an iron red hot and threatened to brand any boy who stepped on the lawn.

The effective leader should keep the following guidelines in mind when it is necessary to change attitudes or behaviour:

1. Be sincere. Do not promise anything that you cannot deliver. Forget about the benefits to yourself and concentrate on the benefits to the other person.
2. Know exactly what it is you want the other person to do.
3. Be empathetic. Ask yourself what is it the other person really wants.

4. Consider the benefits that person will receive from doing what you suggest.
5. Match those benefits to the other person's wants.
6. When you make your request, put it in a form that will convey to the other person the idea that he personally will benefit. We could give a curt order like this, 'John, we have customers coming in tomorrow and I need the stockroom cleaned out. So sweep it out, put the stock in neat piles on the shelves and polish the counter.' Or we could express the same idea by showing John the benefits he will get from doing the task, 'John, we have a job that should be completed right away. If it is done now, we won't be faced with it later. I am bringing some customers in tomorrow to show our facilities. I would like to show them the stockroom, but it is in poor shape. If you could sweep it out, put the stock in neat piles on the shelves and polish the counter, it would make us look efficient and you will have done your part to provide a good company image.'

Will John be happy about doing what you suggest? Probably not very happy, but happier than if you had not pointed out the benefits. Assuming you know that John has pride in the way the stockroom looks and is interested in contributing to the company image, he will be more likely to be cooperative. It also will have been pointed out to John that the job would have to be done eventually and by doing it now, he won't be faced with it later.

It is naïve to believe you will always get a favourable reaction from other persons when you use these approaches, but the experience of most people shows that you are more likely to change attitudes this way than by not using these principles—and if you increase your success by even a mere 10 per cent, you have become 10 per cent more effective as a leader than you were before—and that is *your* benefit.

POINTS TO REMEMBER

1. Always make the other person happy about doing the thing you suggest.
2. Technique of offering incentives and titles.
3. The guidelines to be an effective leader.

16

GIVE A DOG A GOOD NAME

What do you do when a person who has been a good worker begins to turn in shoddy work? You can fire him or her, but that really doesn't solve anything. You can berate the worker, but this usually causes resentment. Henry Henke, a service manager for a large truck dealership in Lowell, Indiana, had a mechanic whose work had become less than satisfactory. Instead of bawling him out or threatening him, Mr Henke called him into his office and had a heart-to-heart talk with him.

'Bill,' he said, 'you are a fine mechanic. You have been in this line of work for a good number of years. You have repaired many vehicles to the customers' satisfaction. In fact, we've had a number of compliments about the good work you have done. Yet, of late, the time you take to complete each job has been increasing and your work has not been up to your own old standards. Because you have been such an outstanding mechanic in the past, I felt sure you would want to know that I am not happy with this situation, and perhaps jointly we could find some way to correct the problem.'

Bill responded that he hadn't realised he had been falling down in his duties and assured his boss that the work he was getting was not out of his range of expertise and he would try to improve in the future.

Did he do it? You can be sure he did. He once again became a fast and thorough mechanic. With that reputation Mr Henke had given him to live up to, how could he do anything else but turn out work comparable to that which he had done in the past.

'The average person,' said Samuel Vauclain, then president of the Baldwin Locomotive Works, 'can be led readily if you have his or her respect and if you show that you respect that person for some kind of ability.'

In short, if you want to improve a person in a certain respect, act as though that particular trait were already one of his or her outstanding characteristics. Shakespeare said, 'Assume a virtue, if you have it not.' And it might be well to assume and state openly that other people have the virtue you want them to develop. Give them a fine reputation to live up to, and they will make prodigious efforts rather than see you disillusioned.

Georgette Leblanc, in her book *Souvenirs, My life with Maeterlinck*, describes the startling transformation of a humble Belgian Cinderella.

'A servant girl from a neighbouring hotel brought my meals,' she wrote. 'She was called "Marie the Dishwasher" because she had started her career as a scullery assistant. She was a kind of monster, cross-eyed, bandy-legged, poor in flesh and spirit.

'One day, while she was holding my plate of macaroni in her red hand, I said to her point-blank, "Marie, you do not know what treasures are within you."

'Accustomed to holding back her emotion, Marie waited for a few moments, not daring to risk the slightest gesture for fear of a catastrophe. Then she put the dish on the table, sighed and said ingenuously, "Madame, I would never have believed it." She did not doubt, she did not ask a question. She simply went back to the kitchen and repeated what I had said, and such is the force of faith that no one made fun of her. From that day on, she was even given a certain consideration. But the most curious change of all occurred in the humble Marie herself. Believing she was the tabernacle of unseen marvels, she began taking care of her face and body so carefully that her starved youth seemed to bloom and modestly hide her plainness.

'Two months later, she announced her coming marriage with the nephew of the chef. "I'm going to be a lady," she said, and thanked me. A small phrase had changed her entire life.'

Georgette Leblanc had given 'Marie the Dishwasher' a reputation to live up to—and that reputation had transformed her.

Bill Parker, a sales representative for a food company in Daytona Beach, Florida, was very excited about the new line of products his company was introducing and was upset when the manager of a large independent food market turned down the opportunity to carry it in his store. Bill brooded all day over this rejection and decided to return to the store before he went home that evening and try again.

'Jack,' he said, 'since I left this morning, I realised I hadn't given you the entire picture of our new line and I would appreciate some of your time to tell you about the points I omitted. I have respected the fact that you are always willing to listen and are big enough to change your mind when the facts warrant a change.'

Could Jack refuse to give him another hearing? Not with that reputation to live up to.

Excel in Leading People Towards their Goals

One morning Dr Martin Fitzhugh, a dentist in Dublin, Ireland, was shocked when one of his patients pointed out to him that the metal cup holder which she was using to rinse her mouth was not very clean. True, the patient drank from the paper cup, not the holder, but it certainly was not professional to use tarnished equipment.

When the patient left, Dr Fitzhugh retreated to his private office to write a note to Bridgit, the charwoman, who came twice a week to clean his office. He wrote:

My dear Bridgit,

I see you so seldom, I thought I'd take the time to thank you for the fine job of cleaning you've been doing. By the way, I thought I'd mention that since two hours, twice a week, is a very limited amount of time, please feel free to work an extra half hour from time to time if you feel you need to do those 'once-in-a-while' things like polishing the cup holders and the like. I, of course, will pay you for the extra time.

'The next day, when I walked into my office,' Dr Fitzhugh reported, 'my desk had been polished to a mirror-like finish, as had my chair, which I nearly slid out of. When I went into the treatment room, I found the shiniest, cleanest chrome-plated cup holder I had ever seen nestled in its receptacle. I had given my charwoman a fine reputation to live up to, and because of this small gesture she out-performed all her past efforts. How much additional time did she spend on this? That's right—none at all.'

There is an old saying, 'Give a dog a bad name and you may as well hang him.' But give him a good name—and see what happens!

When Mrs Ruth Hopkins, a fourth-grade teacher in Brooklyn, New York, looked at her class roster the first day of school, her excitement and joy of starting a new term was tinged with anxiety. In her class this year she would have Tommy T., the school's most notorious 'bad boy'. His third-grade teacher had constantly complained about Tommy to colleagues, the principal and anyone else who would listen. He was not just mischievous; he caused serious discipline problems in the class, picked fights with the boys, teased the girls, was fresh to the teacher and seemed to get worse as he grew older. His only redeeming feature was his ability to learn rapidly and master the school work easily.

Mrs Hopkins decided to face the 'Tommy problem' immediately. When she greeted her new students, she made little comments to each of them, 'Rose, that's a pretty dress you are wearing,' 'Alicia, I hear you draw beautifully.' When she came to Tommy, she looked him straight in the eyes and said, 'Tommy, I understand you are a natural leader. I'm going to depend on you to help me make this class the best class in the fourth grade this year.' She reinforced this over the first few days by complimenting Tommy on everything he did and commenting on how this showed what a good student he was. With that reputation to live up to, even a nine-year-old couldn't let her down—and he didn't.

POINTS TO REMEMBER

1. An average person can be led readily if you have his or her respect.
2. Provide people with a good reputation to live up to and they will.
3. A good employer lets their employee save face!

17

RIDING THE WINGED HORSE

It is common, among those who deal chiefly with life's practicalities, to think of imagination as having little value in comparison with direct thinking. They smile with tolerance when Emerson says, 'Science does not know its debt to the imagination,' for these are the words of a speculative essayist, a philosopher, a poet. But when Napoleon—the indomitable welder of empires—declares, 'The human race is governed by its imagination,' the authoritative word commands their respect.

Be it remembered, the faculty of forming mental images is as efficient a cog as may be found in the whole mind-machine. True, it must fit into that other vital cog, pure thought, but when it does so it may be questioned which is the more productive of important results for the happiness and well-being of man. This should become more apparent as we go on.

WHAT IS IMAGINATION?

Let us not seek for a definition, for a score of varying ones may be found, but let us grasp this fact: by imagination we mean either the faculty or the process of forming mental images.

The subject-matter of imagination may be really existent in nature, or not at all real, or a combination of both; it may be physical or spiritual, or both—the mental image is at once the most lawless and the most law-abiding child that has ever been born of the mind.

First of all, as its name suggests, the process of imagination—for we are thinking of it now as a process rather than as a faculty—is memory at work. Therefore, we must consider it primarily as

REPRODUCTIVE IMAGINATION

We see or hear or feel or taste or smell something and the sensation passes away. Yet we are conscious of a greater or lesser ability to reproduce such feelings at will. Two considerations, in general, will govern the vividness of the image thus evoked—the strength of the original impression, and the reproductive power of one mind as compared with another. Yet every normal person will be able to evoke images with some degree of clearness.

The fact that not all minds possess this imaging faculty in anything like equal measure will have an important bearing on the public speaker's study of this question. No man who does not feel at least some poetic impulses is likely to aspire seriously to be a poet, yet many whose imaging faculties are so dormant as to seem actually dead do aspire to be public speakers. To all such we say most earnestly: awaken your image-making gift, for even in the most coldly logical discourse it is sure to prove of great service. It is important that you find out at once just how full and how trustworthy is your imagination, for it is capable of cultivation—as well as of abuse.

Francis Galton says:

> The French appear to possess the visualizing faculty in a high degree. The peculiar ability they show in pre-

arranging ceremonials and fêtes of all kinds and their undoubted genius for tactics and strategy show that they are able to foresee effects with unusual clearness. Their ingenuity in all technical contrivances is an additional testimony in the same direction, and so is their singular clearness of expression. Their phrase 'figurez-vous', or picture to yourself, seems to express their dominant mode of perception. Our equivalent, of 'image', is ambiguous.

But individuals differ in this respect just as markedly as, for instance, the Dutch do from the French. And this is true not only of those who are classified by their friends as being respectively imaginative or unimaginative, but of those whose gifts or habits are not well known.

Let us take for experiment six of the best-known types of imaging and see in practice how they arise in our own minds.

By all odds the most common type is,

(a) the visual image: children who more readily recall things seen than things heard are called by psychologists 'eye-minded', and most of us are bent in this direction. Close your eyes now and re-call—the word thus hyphenated is more suggestive—the scene around this morning's breakfast table. Possibly there was nothing striking in the situation and the image is therefore not striking. Then image any notable table scene in your experience—how vividly it stands forth, because at the time you felt the impression strongly. Just then you may not have been conscious of how strongly the scene was laying hold upon you, for often we are so intent upon what we see that we give no particular thought to the fact that it is impressing us. It may surprise you to learn how accurately you are able to image a scene when a long time has elapsed between the conscious focussing of your attention on the image and the time when you saw the original.

(b) The auditory image is probably the next most vivid of our recalled experiences. Here association is potent to suggest similarities. Close out all the world beside and listen to the peculiar wood-against-wood sound of the sharp thunder among rocky mountains—the crash of ball against ten-pins may suggest it. Or image (the word is imperfect, for it seems to suggest only the eye) the sound of tearing ropes when some precious weight hangs in danger. Or recall the bay of a hound almost upon you in pursuit—choose your own sound, and see how pleasantly or terribly real it becomes when imaged in your brain.

(c) The motor image is a close competitor with the auditory for second place. Have you ever awakened in the night, every muscle taut and striving, to feel yourself straining against the opposing football line that held like a stonewall—or as firmly as the headboard of your bed? Or voluntarily recall the movement of the boat when you cried inwardly, 'It's all up with me!' The perilous lurch of a train, the sudden sinking of an elevator or the unexpected toppling of a rocking-chair may serve as further experiments.

(d) The gustatory image is common enough, as the idea of eating lemons will testify. Sometimes the pleasurable recollection of a delightful dinner will cause the mouth to water years afterward, or the 'image' of particularly atrocious medicine will wrinkle the nose long after it made one day in boyhood wretched.

(e) The olfactory image is even more delicate. Some there

are who are affected to illness by the memory of certain odours, while others experience the most delectable sensations by the rise of pleasing olfactory images.

(f) The tactile image, to name no others, is well-nigh as potent. Do you shudder at the thought of velvet rubbed by short-nailed fingertips? Or were you ever 'burned' by touching an ice-cold stove? Or, happier memory, can you still feel the touch of a well-loved absent hand?

Be it remembered that few of these images are present in our minds except in combination—the sight and sound of the crashing avalanche are one; so are the flash and report of the huntsman's gun that came so near 'doing for us'.

Thus, imaging—especially conscious reproductive imagination—will become a valuable part of our mental processes in proportion as we direct and control it.

PRODUCTIVE IMAGINATION

All of the foregoing examples, and doubtless also many of the experiments you yourself may originate, are merely reproductive. Pleasurable or horrific as these may be, they are far less important than the images evoked by the productive imagination—though that does not infer a separate faculty.

Recall, again for experiment, some scene whose beginning you once saw enacted on a street corner but passed by before the dénouement was ready to be disclosed. Recall it all—that far the image is reproductive. But what followed? Let your fantasy roam at pleasure—the succeeding scenes are productive, for you have more or less consciously invented the unreal on the basis of the real.

And just here the fictionist, the poet and the public speaker will see the value of productive imagery. True, the feet of the idol you build are on the ground, but its head pierces the clouds, it is a son of both earth and heaven.

One fact is important to note here: imagery is a valuable mental asset in proportion as it is controlled by the higher intellectual power of pure reason. The untutored child of nature thinks largely in images and therefore attaches to them undue importance. He readily confuses the real with the unreal—to him they are of like value. But the man of training readily distinguishes the one from the other and evaluates each with some, if not with perfect, justice.

So we see that unrestrained imaging may produce a rudderless steamer, while the trained faculty is the graceful sloop, skimming the seas at her skipper's will, her course steadied by the helm of reason and her lightsome wings catching every air of heaven.

The game of chess, the war lord's tactical plan, the evolution of a geometrical theorem, the devising of a great business campaign, the elimination of waste in a factory, the dénouement of a powerful drama, the overcoming of an economic obstacle, the scheme for a sublime poem and the convincing siege of an audience may—nay, indeed must—each be conceived in an image and wrought to reality according to the plans and specifications laid upon the trestle board by some modern imaginative Hiram. The farmer who would be content with the seed he possesses would have no harvest. Do not rest satisfied with the ability to recall images, but cultivate your creative imagination by building 'what might be' upon the foundation of 'what is'.

The Uses of Imaging in Public Speaking

By this time you will have already made some general application of these ideas to the art of the platform, but to several specific uses we must now refer.

I. IMAGING IN SPEECH-PREPARATION

(a) Set the image of your audience before you while you prepare. Disappointment may lurk here, and you cannot be forearmed for every emergency, but in the main you must meet your audience before you actually do—image its probable mood and attitude toward the occasion, the theme and the speaker.

(b) Conceive your speech as a whole while you are preparing its parts, else you cannot see—image—how its parts shall be fitly framed together.

(c) Image the language you will use, so far as written or extemporaneous speech may dictate. The habit of imaging will give you choice of varied figures of speech, for remember that an address without fresh comparisons is like a garden without blooms. Do not be content with the first hackneyed figure that comes flowing to your pen-point, but dream on until the striking, the unusual, yet the vividly real comparison points your thought like steel does the arrow-tip.

Note the freshness and effectiveness of the following description from the opening of O. Henry's story, 'The Harbinger'.

> Long before the springtide is felt in the dull bosom of the yokel does the city man know that the grass-green goddess is upon her throne. He sits at his breakfast eggs and toast, begirt by stone walls, opens his morning paper and sees journalism leave vernalism at the post.
>
> For whereas Spring's couriers were once the evidence of our finer senses, now the Associated Press does the trick.
>
> The warble of the first robin in Hackensack, the stirring of the maple sap in Bennington, the budding

of the pussy willows along the main street in Syracuse, the first chirp of the bluebird, the swansong of the blue point, the annual tornado in St. Louis, the plaint of the peace pessimist from Pompton, N.J., the regular visit of the tame wild goose with a broken leg to the pond near Bilgewater Junction, the base attempt of the Drug Trust to boost the price of quinine foiled in the House by Congressman Jinks, the first tall poplar struck by lightning and the usual stunned picknickers who had taken refuge, the first crack of the ice jamb in the Allegheny River, the finding of a violet in its mossy bed by the correspondent at Round Corners—these are the advanced signs of the burgeoning season that are wired into the wise city, while the farmer sees nothing but winter upon his dreary fields.

But these be mere externals. The true harbinger is the heart. When Strephon seeks his Chloe, and Mike his Maggie, then only is Spring arrived and the newspaper report of the five-foot rattler killed in Squire Pettregrew's pasture confirmed.

A hackneyed writer would probably have said that the newspaper told the city man about spring before the farmer could see any evidence of it, but that the real harbinger of spring was love and that, 'In the Spring a young man's fancy lightly turns to thoughts of love.'

II. IMAGING IN SPEECH-DELIVERY

When once the passion of speech is on you and you are 'warmed up'—perhaps by striking till the iron is hot so that you may not fail to strike when it is hot—your mood will be one of vision.

Then:

(a) Re-image past emotion—of which more elsewhere. The actor re-calls the old feelings every time he renders his telling lines.
(b) Reconstruct in image the scenes you are to describe.
(c) Image the objects in nature whose tone you are delineating, so that bearing and voice and movement (gesture) will picture forth the whole convincingly. Instead of merely stating the fact that whiskey ruins homes, the temperance speaker paints a drunkard coming home to abuse his wife and strike his children. It is much more effective than telling the truth in abstract terms. To depict the cruelness of war, do not assert the fact abstractly: 'War is cruel.' Show the soldier, an arm swept away by a bursting shell, lying on the battlefield pleading for water; show the children with tear-stained faces pressed against the window pane praying for their dead father to return. Avoid general and prosaic terms. Paint pictures. Evolve images for the imagination of your audience to construct into pictures of their own.

III. HOW TO ACQUIRE THE IMAGING HABIT

You remember the American statesman who asserted that 'the way to resume is to resume'? The application is obvious. Beginning with the first simple analyses of this chapter, test your own qualities of image-making. One by one practice the several kinds of images; then add—even invent—others in combination, for many images come to us in complex form, like the combined noise and shoving and hot odour of a cheering crowd.

After practising on reproductive imaging, turn to the productive, beginning with the reproductive and adding productive features for the sake of cultivating invention.

Frequently, allow your originating gifts full swing by weaving complete imaginary fabrics—sights, sounds, scenes; all the fine world of fantasy lies open to the journeyings of your winged steed.

In like manner train yourself in the use of figurative language. Learn first to distinguish and then to use its varied forms. When used with restraint, nothing can be more effective than the trope; but once let extravagance creep in by the window, and power will flee by the door.

All in all, master your images—let not them master you.

POINTS TO REMEMBER

1. The human race is governed by its imagination.
2. Awaken your imaginative gift, for even in the most coldly logical discourse it is sure to prove of great service.
3. Significance of conscious reproductive imagination for our mental processes.

18

TEAMING UP FOR TOMORROW

It used to be that big organizations were shaped like pyramids. They had many workers on the bottom and layer after layer of supervisors and middle managers above. Each layer had more authority than the one beneath it. And this multi-layered structure rose ever so neatly to a perfect, predictable point—where the CEO, the chairman and the board of directors got to sit.

Was this the best way to organize a company, a hospital, a school? Almost no one ever bothered to ask. The old pyramid was as it always had been: solid, impressive and seemingly impervious to change.

Now this might come as a surprise to some people, but the pyramids are tumbling down. It's as if the slaves of ancient Egypt decided to return and they're carting away the stones. The new landscape may never be as flat as the sandy Sahara. But you can bet the future will be a whole lot more horizontal than the past.

All those rigid hierarchies, all those departmental lines, all those intricate chains of command—all of it stifled creative work. And who can afford that when the world is changing so fast?

'Look at what happened to the former USSR as a hierarchy,'

says Richard C. Bartlett, vice chairman of the Mary Kay Corporation. 'The same thing will probably happen to China because of hierarchy. It doesn't work for governments. It doesn't work for corporations either. The biggest corporations we've got in the United States didn't even notice the world coming down around their ears.'

Clearly what's been needed is a structure that loosens up the old rigidity, that could let people do their creative best, that could fully develop the talent that's been lying dormant for years. In more and more well-led organizations, the answer is being found in teams. Increasingly often, people are being asked to work beyond their disciplines, outside their cultures, above and below their usual ranks.

'The modern organization cannot be an organization of boss and subordinate,' argues business theorist Peter Drucker, professor of management at the Claremont Graduate School in California. 'It must be organized as a team.'

Andrés Navarro, president of Chile's SONDA, S.A., agrees. 'The Lone Ranger is no longer possible,' Navarro observes. 'A guy by himself inventing something alone—the world is too complicated for that. You need several people from different disciplines working together at the same time.'

Small groups of people, recruited from throughout the organization, brought together for ongoing projects or for some specific, limited task—to design a new product, to reorganize a plant, to restructure a department, to figure out how to add momentum to a quality-improvement program. Fading are the old departmental rivalries. And fading are the automatic promotions, the seniority-based pay scales and the other frustrating vestiges of the old pyramid.

In pyramid companies, the engineers spent all day cooped up with other engineers. Now an engineer might just as easily be thrown into a group of salespeople and told, 'Help make this product more attractive to the customer.' Or 'Figure out how to build that part faster.' Or 'Use your engineering expertise to guide this marketing group around a technical glitch.'

As a result of groupings like this, marketing is actually listening to engineering and engineering is listening back. At many big companies this never, ever happened before. And now manufacturing, customer service, labour relations and all the other far-flung departments are communicating too. At some progressive companies, these entire artificial divisions are even beginning to disappear.

As Drucker argues, the world is not made up of privates and drill sergeants anymore. 'The army was organized by command-and-control, and business enterprise as well as most other institutions copied that model,' he writes. 'This is now rapidly changing. As more and more organizations become information-based, they are transforming themselves into soccer or tennis teams—that is, into responsibility-based organizations in which every member must act as a responsible decision-maker. All members have to see themselves as executives.'

Look at how the Mary Kay Corporation is organized. 'The Mary Kay organizational structure is a free form,' says Vice Chairman Richard Bartlett. 'I like to think of it almost as a molecular structure, where people can go right through any artificial barriers. They are not confined to a box. They can participate in a creative action team right across departmental lines. And in our view of the world—and this sounds trite to say, but a few people have jumped on the bandwagon since—the customer is right smack on top.

'But in the way we do business, right below her [the customer] is our sales force. Our organization is very focused on how to support that sales force. At the bottom of the organizational chart is something that is referred to as an insignificant green dot.

'The first time I ever did a slide presentation on how to structure an organization, the artist put a green dot down there,' Bartlett recalls. 'I'm the insignificant green dot. My personal view of the world is that there is no need for a president or chairman unless he is dedicated to serving the needs of others and to providing resources to the people who are getting the job done.'

'Organizations are actually restructuring,' says Adele Scheele, whose articles on career-management issues appear regularly in American and Japanese business magazines. 'What used to work no longer works. People expected there would be a set path, and there is no set path. So the more you believe in that, the less likely you are to be able to be flexible and begin to take advantage of opportunities that never come labelled. You want to always be open.'

These flattened organizations are turning up in all kinds of surprising places, even in the educational world. 'Management is becoming a lot flatter,' observes Marc Horowitz, principal of Cantiague Elementary School in Jericho, New York. 'And there's a real need to build teams, lead teams and motivate people horizontally. In many cases it has to be done without title, without financial remuneration or incentive. It's the team's performance that's key.'

What this means in Horowitz's school is that students no longer work by themselves all day long in rows of wooden desks. They cooperate. They work in teams. They produce group projects. The students are expected to help each other. The teachers also work more cooperatively than they ever have before. 'Now it's "How do we relate together and get results in the real world?"' Horowitz explains. 'We're preparing students for the future. They really can't work in isolation anymore. They have to get involved in a team effort, and half of that battle is learning the social skills to encourage those in the group who aren't doing so well. They should never be allowed to feel less than worthy because they slip up or they do not have all the answers.'

Three first-graders at Horowitz's school were involved in a group project one day. One of the children had the task of writing the word two on a piece of paper. But the child misspelled the word, writing it as tow. When a girl in the group pointed out the error, the boy felt bad for a moment. But then the little girl said, 'Don't worry about it. I know you misspelled it. But that was a beautiful w, okay?' She even gave him a pat on the knee, and all three of the students got a good lesson in working cooperatively.

The Harvard Business School's marketing faculty recently conducted a teamwork experiment with the first-year graduate students. Instead of the usual midterm case-study exam, these students were divided at random into teams of four. Each team was given a business problem to solve—and twenty-four hours to come back with a written plan. The members of each team would get the same grade.

'Initially there was much criticism,' says John Quelch, the Harvard business school professor. 'Some students complained that individual grades would be adversely affected by the fact that they were thrown into a team with a group of people they wouldn't have selected to work with.' The school's answer: welcome to the real world.

In the end, the Harvard students came around. When the student newspaper surveyed the students after the experience, they expressed an overwhelming support for the new group-project midterm exam.

'The most significant level of learning,' Quelch says, 'was probably among students in those groups that did not perform like clockwork. There were some groups which experienced tremendous disagreements, and in retrospect, those were the students who learned the most out of the whole process.'

Effective teamwork doesn't happen by magic. It takes a cooperative group of players, and it takes a talented coach. You can't simply throw a few individuals together—even a few highly talented individuals—and expect them to perform brilliantly.

That's why the National Basketball Association all-star game so often falls short of its hype. Sure, the game features many of the finest players in America, brought together on a single basketball court. Pound for pound, there is no more talented collection of guards, forwards and centres anywhere. So why does this floor full of phenomenal talent so seldom produce a phenomenal game?

Too much ego. Too much time in the spotlight. Too many mornings on the sports page. When it comes to playing as part of a unit, these superstars often fail to measure up. The missing ingredient is teamwork.

There is an art to building successful teams, and even a great coach can rarely mould a winner overnight. But anyone who expects to be a leader in the years to come had better master a few basic coaching techniques. They are as necessary in the business world as they are on the basketball court.

CREATE A SHARED SENSE OF PURPOSE

People working together can accomplish tremendous things.

What gives a team that special boost is the unified vision the individual members share.

The ideas, the creativity, the intelligent sparks will ultimately have to come from the group itself. But a strong leader is often needed to focus all that energy—to clarify the vision, to establish goals, to help everyone understand what the team is about, to show the team members how their accomplishments will impact upon the outside world.

Ray Stata, chairman of Analog Devices Inc., says, 'You've got to provide the environment, the corporate objective and the encouragement so that people as individuals and as teams of individuals can feel that they're world-class, that they are better than any other team and that there's recognition and feedback which acknowledges that.'

MAKE THE GOALS TEAM-GOALS

Unless the whole team wins, no one wins. This concept is most familiar in the world of sports, but it's just as true for teams of any sort. Individual records are fine for the history books, but really, they're an afterthought. What matters far more is the performance of the entire team.

'When you get people involved in this way and they feed off each other, it's contagious,' says Rubbermaid's Wolfgang Schmitt. 'It becomes a lot more like being a member of a sports team versus being in an assembly line. There's just a big difference in the energy level they bring into the work, the intensity.'

That's why most good coaches—and most good leaders—speak so often in the first-person plural: 'We need...', 'Our deadline...', 'The job before us...' Good leaders always emphasize how everyone's contribution fits in.

In business, 'Together we have to get this new product smoothly to market.' If the ad man does marvellous work but the packaging specialist fails, that's not success.

In sailing, 'Together we have to get this boat through the storm.' If the navigator can read the stars like a paperback novel but the skipper doesn't know the difference between starboard and port, that's not success.

In politics, 'Together we have to win this election.' If the candidate is a splendid orator but the advance staff can't get her to the speech, that's not success.

TREAT PEOPLE LIKE THE INDIVIDUALS THEY ARE

When individuals come together as a team, their individuality doesn't suddenly evaporate. They still have different personalities. They still have different skills. They still have different hopes and fears. A talented leader will recognize those differences, appreciate them and use them to the advantage of the team.

Individually—that's how Bela Karolyi, the internationally renowned gymnastics coach, prepared his students for the Olympic Games. 'If I wasn't producing what he wanted,' recalls Olympic gold medallist Mary Lou Retton, a star student of Karolyi's, 'he would ignore me. I'd rather him yell at me, I swear.' But Karolyi was smart enough to recognize that that approach was exactly what Retton needed.

'I would do a vault,' she recalls. 'I'd put my hands up, and then I'd turn around. He would be looking down at the next girl, who was ready to go. Oh, I wanted his attention so much. I wanted him to say, "That was good, Mary Lou." He would use that to get results out of me, and that would push me to make the correction, to get that praise.'

Was Karolyi just a grouch? Not at all. With other students he took an entirely different tack. Retton will never forget the approach Karolyi used on teammate Julianne McNamara. 'She has a much different personality than I do,' Retton says. 'She's much more timid, a little reserved. He would be very gentle with her. If she wasn't making that correction, he'd come and put her body where it needed to be and talk quietly to her. He was always much more gentle with her. That's how he got personal results.

'He treated each student differently, and I think that's very important.'

MAKE EACH MEMBER RESPONSIBLE FOR THE TEAM PRODUCT

People need to feel their contributions are important. Otherwise, they'll devote less than complete attention to the tasks at hand.

Make the project belong to the team. Let as many decisions as possible bubble up from the group. Invite participation. Don't dictate solutions. Don't insist that things be done a certain way.

The Jaycraft Corporation had a problem. Its biggest customer had a giant order—and a delivery date that seemed impossible to meet. Doug Van Vechten, the company president, could have imposed a solution from the top.

But he knew better than to try. Instead, he asked a team of his employees to figure out what to do. 'They came back to me and said, "We can move some things around here and there, and we feel that we can do it, and let's take the job,"' Van Vechten remembers. Jaycraft took the job and met the customer's delivery demand.

SHARE THE GLORY, ACCEPT THE BLAME

When the team does well and is recognized, it's the leader's responsibility to spread the benefits around. A public pat on the back, a bonus from the top, a write-up in the company magazine—whatever form that recognition takes, everyone should get a generous share of it.

Denis Potvin, former captain of the New York Islanders hockey team, knew how to share the glory when his team won the Stanley Cup. But just in case he didn't, coach Al Arbour knew enough about team play to remind him. 'Make sure you let the other guys carry the cup,' the coach whispered into Potvin's ear, a few seconds after the final buzzer of the championship game.

'He came on the ice and rushed over to the pile of celebrating Islanders,' Potvin explains. 'We're all congratulating each other. I turned, and Al was there. We both hugged one another. And it was there, in my ear, that he told me that.

'I was very impressed,' Potvin recalls. 'Here is a guy who is in total control of the team. He was still thinking about his players even though the Stanley Cup had just been won—his first time as a coach.'

People always appreciate being included in praise. It encourages them to give their greatest efforts and makes them want to work again with the leader who guided them to this success. And this kind of graciousness has one other benefit: in the end the leader gets a big share of the credit anyway.

When it comes to criticism, be a smart leader and take exactly the opposite approach. Don't point the finger at others. Never raise public complaints about the 'weak link' in the chain. Step forward and accept whatever complaints arrive. Then speak privately with the team members about how the results might be improved, and turn their attention to doing better next time.

TAKE EVERY OPPORTUNITY TO BUILD CONFIDENCE ON THE TEAM

A great leader will believe firmly in the team and will share that belief with every member.

That's a lesson kindergarten teacher Barbara Hammerman puts into action in her classroom, and it applies just as well in the factory or boardroom. 'I try to build a class spirit within the room,' she says. 'To the children in my class, we are the best class, and there is a feeling that we don't want to disappoint the group—one for all and all for one—that we have certain standards that are set and reviewed and continuously reinforced through the year. The children understand these standards.'

They aren't intimidated by them. 'They just love living up to these standards because we're great,' Hammerman said. 'Who doesn't want to feel as if they're part of the wonderful group? When they get compliments from others, they can begin to see the progress they are making and changes in themselves. And they just feel wonderful about themselves.'

BE INVOLVED, STAY INVOLVED

In those old pyramid companies, it was easy for the boss to remain relatively aloof. After all, that army of minions was always hovering around, just waiting to distribute the boss's latest wisdom to the troops.

This approach doesn't fly in the new team-based world. The strong leader has to be involved and stay involved. Visualize the leader as the commander of a busy aircraft carrier, standing out on deck. Planes are coming in. Others are taking off. The ship has to stay on course and also be protected from attack. All these considerations have to be factored in together.

The leader really does have to *be there*. 'You've got to have the experience, and you've got to listen,' says Jack Gallagher, president of North Shore University Hospital in Manhasset, New York. 'But after a while, if you get enough experience, if you work hard enough, if you're smart enough, if you do your homework, then you get a good feel for all these planes going up and down and for all the other things around you.'

'You can't always draw up a precise battle plan.

'You've got to get an intuitive feel for it, and you've got to have antennae out, the antennae in the back of your head,' Gallagher says. 'Sure, there are too many things going on and this is a very complex business. But you can develop that intuitive feel.'

BE A MENTOR

It's the leader's job to develop the talents and strengthen the people on the team. This is true in the short term, as the team members deal with their assignment at hand. But it's also true long-term: the leaders must take a genuine responsibility for the lives and careers of the members of the team.

'How would you like to improve?' 'Where do you want your career to go from here?' 'What kinds of new responsibilities would you like to be taking on?' It's your job as leader to ask all those questions and to use whatever knowledge and experience you possess to help team members achieve those goals.

Reinforce the confidence you have in their abilities. Give them standards to live up to. Issue genuine compliments in public: 'Sally has done a terrific job on this report.' Send private notes: 'That was a great comment you made today. You got us all focused where we needed to be.' And remember, if they succeed, you succeed.

At Harvard University's Graduate School of Business Administration, new faculty members aren't just left to sink or swim.

'All seven or eight instructors teaching our introductory marketing course meet every week for four hours as a group to discuss the cases that are coming up and how best to teach those cases,' says Professor John Quelch. 'They also review how the cases went the previous week, what improvements need to be made, and so forth. In this way, newly recruited instructors can pick up teaching tips from our more experienced faculty.'

The senior faculty members also provide other kinds of support. Three or four times a semester, one of them sits in on a new instructor's class. They come to help, not to judge. 'They're there very much in a coaching role,' Quelch explains, 'rather than to develop a report for a file that's going to determine your promotion. The goal is to enhance the effectiveness of the asset—the new faculty member—that we've invested in.'

After class the senior faculty member might provide advice for both short- and long-term improvement. 'What I would try to say to a new faculty member,' Quelch continues, 'is, "Here are five things you can do the next time you teach that will have a positive impact on the way you're received by the class." Suggestions might include, for example, something as seemingly trivial as writing larger on the blackboard. Or 'Make sure that you don't hang around the blackboard and direct the class from one area at the front of the room. Wander around the entire room and stand behind the students. Share the experience.'

As Walter Lippmann wrote upon the death of Franklin Delano Roosevelt, 'The final test of a leader is that he leaves behind him in other men the conviction and the will to carry on.'

Follow these few simple techniques and watch how your

team succeeds. The greatest reward a leader can achieve—the greatest legacy a leader can leave—is a group of talented, self-confident and cooperative people, who are themselves ready to lead.

TEAM PLAYERS ARE THE LEADERS OF TOMORROW.

POINTS TO REMEMBER

1. Hollowness of the pyramid structure of an organization.
2. A modern workplace can't be a place of boss and subordinate. But of a team.
3. A team's special boost is the unified vision the individual members share.

19

IF YOU MUST FIND FAULT, THIS IS THE WAY TO BEGIN

A friend of mine was a guest at the White House for a weekend during the administration of Calvin Coolidge. Drifting into the President's private office, he heard Coolidge say to one of his secretaries, 'That's a very pretty dress you are wearing this morning, and you are a very attractive young woman.'

That was probably the most effusive praise Silent Cal had ever bestowed upon a secretary in his life. It was so unusual, so unexpected, that the secretary blushed in confusion. Then Coolidge said, 'Now, don't get stuck up. I just said that to make you feel good. From now on, I wish you would be a little more careful with your punctuation.'

His method was probably a bit obvious, but the psychology was superb. It is always easier to listen to unpleasant things after we have heard some praise of our good points.

A barber lathers a man before he shaves him; and that is precisely what McKinley did back in 1896, when he was running for President. One of the prominent Republicans of that day had written a campaign speech that he felt was just a trifle better than Cicero and Patrick Henry and Daniel Webster all rolled into one. With great glee, this chap read his immortal speech aloud to McKinley. The speech had its fine points, but it just wouldn't do. McKinley didn't want to hurt the man's feelings. He must not kill the man's splendid enthusiasm, and yet he had to say 'no'. Note how adroitly he did it.

'My friend, that is a splendid speech, a magnificent speech,' McKinley said. 'No one could have prepared a better one. There are many occasions on which it would be precisely the right thing to say, but is it quite suitable to this particular occasion? Sound and sober as it is from your standpoint, I must consider its effect from the party's standpoint. Now go home and write a speech along the lines I indicate, and send me a copy of it.'

He did just that. McKinley blue-pencilled and helped him rewrite his second speech, and he became one of the effective speakers of the campaign.

Here is the second most famous letter that Abraham Lincoln ever wrote. (His most famous one was written to Mrs Bixby, expressing his sorrow for the death of the five sons she had lost in battle.) Lincoln probably dashed this letter off in five minutes; yet it sold at public auction in 1926 for $12,000, and that, by the way, was more money than Lincoln was able to save during half a century of hard work. The letter was written to General Joseph Hooker on 26 April 1863, during the darkest period of the Civil War. For eighteen months, Lincoln's generals had been leading the Union Army from one tragic defeat to another. Nothing but futile, stupid human butchery. The nation was appalled. Thousands of soldiers had deserted from the army and even the Republican members of the Senate had revolted and wanted to force Lincoln out of the White House. 'We are now on the brink of destruction,' Lincoln said. 'It appears to me that even the Almighty is against us. I can hardly see a ray of hope.' Such was the period of black sorrow and chaos out of which this letter came.

I am printing the letter here because it shows how Lincoln tried to change an obstreperous general when the very fate of the nation could have depended upon the general's action.

This is perhaps the sharpest letter Abe Lincoln wrote after he became President; yet you will note that he praised General Hooker before he spoke of his grave faults.

Yes, they were grave faults, but Lincoln didn't call them that. Lincoln was more conservative, more diplomatic. Lincoln wrote, 'There are some things in regard to which I am not quite satisfied with you.' Talk about tact! And diplomacy!

Here is the letter addressed to General Hooker:

> I have placed you at the head of the Army of the Potomac. Of course, I have done this upon what appears to me to be sufficient reasons, and yet I think it best for you to know that there are some things in regard to which I am not quite satisfied with you.
>
> I believe you to be a brave and skilful soldier, which, of course, I like. I also believe you do not mix politics with your profession, in which you are right. You have confidence in yourself, which is a valuable if not an indispensable quality.
>
> You are ambitious, which, within reasonable bounds, does good rather than harm. But I think that during General Burnside's command of the army you have taken counsel of your ambition and thwarted him as much as you could, in which you did a great wrong to the country and to a most meritorious and honourable brother officer.
>
> I have heard, in such a way as to believe it, of your recently saying that both the army and the Government needed a dictator. Of course, it was not for this, but in spite of it, that I have given you command.

Only those generals who gain successes can set up as dictators. What I now ask of you is military success and I will risk the dictatorship.

The Government will support you to the utmost of its ability, which is neither more nor less than it has done and will do for all commanders. I much fear that the spirit which you have aided to infuse into the army, of criticising their commander and withholding confidence from him, will now turn upon you. I shall assist you, as far as I can, to put it down.

Neither you nor Napoleon, if he were alive again, could get any good out of an army while such spirit prevails in it, and now beware of rashness. Beware of rashness, but with energy and sleepless vigilance, go forward and give us victories.

You are not a Coolidge, a McKinley or a Lincoln. You want to know whether this philosophy will operate for you in everyday business contacts. Will it? Let's see. Let's take the case of W.P. Gaw, of the Wark Company, Philadelphia.

The Wark Company had contracted to build and complete a large office building in Philadelphia by a certain specified date. Everything was going along well; the building was almost finished, when suddenly the subcontractor making the ornamental bronze work to go on the exterior of this building declared that he couldn't make delivery on schedule. What! An entire building held up! Heavy penalties! Distressing losses! All because of one man!

Long-distance telephone calls. Arguments! Heated conversations! All in vain. Then Mr Gaw was sent to New York to beard the bronze lion in his den.

'Do you know you are the only person in Brooklyn with

your name?' Mr Gaw asked the president of the subcontracting firm shortly after they were introduced. The president was surprised. 'No, I didn't know that.'

'Well,' said Mr Gaw, 'when I got off the train this morning, I looked in the telephone book to get your address, and you're the only person in the Brooklyn phone book with your name.'

'I never knew that,' the subcontractor said. He checked the phone book with interest. 'Well, it's an unusual name,' he said proudly. 'My family came from Holland and settled in New York almost two hundred years ago.' He continued to talk about his family and his ancestors for several minutes. When he finished that, Mr Gaw complimented him on how large a plant he had and compared it favourably with a number of similar plants he had visited. 'It is one of the cleanest and neatest bronze factories I ever saw,' said Gaw.

'I've spent a lifetime building up this business,' the subcontractor said, 'and I am rather proud of it. Would you like to take a look around the factory?'

During this tour of inspection, Mr Gaw complimented the other man on his system of fabrication and told him how and why it seemed superior to those of some of his competitors. Gaw commented on some unusual machines, and the subcontractor announced that he himself had invented those machines. He spent considerable time showing Gaw how they operated and the superior work they turned out. He insisted on taking his visitor to lunch. So far, mind you, not a word had been said about the real purpose of Gaw's visit.

After lunch, the subcontractor said, 'Now, to get down to business. Naturally, I know why you're here. I didn't expect that our meeting would be so enjoyable. You can go back to Philadelphia with my promise that your material will be fabricated and shipped, even if other orders have to be delayed.'

Mr Gaw got everything that he wanted without even asking for it. The material arrived on time and the building was completed on the day the completion contract specified.

Would this have happened had Mr Gaw used the hammer-and-dynamite method generally employed on such occasions?

Dorothy Wrublewski, a branch manager of the Fort Monmouth, New Jersey, Federal Credit Union, reported to one of our classes how she was able to help one of her employees become more productive.

'We recently hired a young lady as a teller trainee. Her contact with our customers was very good. She was accurate and efficient in handling individual transactions. The problem developed at the end of the day when it was time to balance out.

'The head teller came to me and strongly suggested that I fire this woman. "She is holding up everyone else because she is so slow in balancing out. I've shown her over and over, but she can't get it. She's got to go."

'The next day I observed her working quickly and accurately when handling the normal everyday transactions, and she was very pleasant with our customers.

'It didn't take long to discover why she had trouble balancing out. After the office closed, I went over to talk with her. She was obviously nervous and upset. I praised her for being so friendly and outgoing with the customers and complimented her for the accuracy and speed used in that work. I then suggested we review the procedure we use in balancing the cash drawer. Once she realized I had confidence in her, she easily followed my suggestions and soon mastered this function. We have had no problems with her since then.'

Beginning with praise is like the dentist who begins his work with Novocain. The patient still gets a drilling, but the Novocain is pain-killing. A leader will use...

POINTS TO REMEMBER

1. It is always easier to listen to unpleasant things after we have heard some praise of our good points.
2. There are a thousand ways to say 'no'.
3. Your trust is the best gift you can give to someone.

20

FIND YOURSELF AND BE YOURSELF

I have a letter from Mrs. Edith Allred, of Mount Airy, North Carolina, 'As a child, I was extremely sensitive and shy,' she says in her letter. 'I was always overweight and my cheeks made me look even fatter than I was. I had an old-fashioned mother who thought it was foolish to make clothes look pretty. She always said, "Wide will wear while narrow will tear", and she dressed me accordingly. I never went parties; never had any fun; and when I went to school, I never joined the other children in outside activities, not even athletics. I was morbidly shy. I felt I was "different" from everybody else and entirely undesirable.

'When I grew up, I married a man who was several years my senior. But I didn't change. My in-laws were a poised and self-confident family. They were everything I should have been but simply was not. I tried my best to be like them, but I couldn't. Every attempt they made to draw me out of myself only drove me further into my shell. I became nervous and irritable. I avoided all friends. I got so bad I even dreaded the sound of the doorbell ringing! I was a failure. I knew it; and I was afraid my husband would find it out. So, whenever we were in public, I tried to be gay and overacted my part. I knew I overacted; and I would be miserable for days afterwards. At last I became so unhappy that I could see no point in prolonging my existence. I began to think of suicide.'

What happened to change this unhappy woman's life? Just a chance remark!

'A chance remark,' Mrs. Allred continued, 'transformed my whole life. My mother-in-law was talking one day of how she brought her children up, and she said, "No matter what happened, I always insisted on their being themselves." "...on being themselves." ...That remark is what did it! In a flash, I realized I had brought all this misery on myself by trying to fit myself into a pattern to which I did not conform.

'I changed overnight! I started being myself. I tried to make a study of my own personality. Tried to find out *what I was.* I studied my strong points. I learned all I could about colours and styles and dressed in a way that I felt was becoming to me. I reached out to make friends. I joined an organization—a small one at first—and was petrified with fright when they put me on a program. But each time I spoke, I gained a little courage. It took a long while—but today I have more happiness than I ever dreamed possible. In rearing my own children, I have always taught them the lesson I had to learn from such bitter experience: *No matter what happens, always be yourself!*'

This problem of being unwilling to be yourself is 'as old as history', says Dr. James Gordon Gilkey, 'and as universal as human life.' This problem of being unwilling to be yourself is the hidden spring behind many neuroses and psychoses and complexes. Angelo Patri has written thirteen books and thousands of syndicated newspaper articles on the subject of child training, and he says, 'Nobody is so miserable as he who longs to be somebody and something other than the person he is in body and mind.'

This craving to be something you are not is especially rampant in Hollywood. Sam Wood, one of Hollywood's best-known directors, said the greatest headache he has with aspiring young actors is exactly this problem: to make them be themselves. They all want to be second-rate Lana Turners or third-rate Clark Gables. 'The public has already had that flavour,' Sam Wood keeps telling them; 'now it wants something else.'

Before he started directing such pictures as *Goodbye, Mr. Chips* and *For Whom the Bell Tolls,* Sam Wood spent years in the real-estate business, developing sales personalities. He declares that the same principles apply in the business world as in the world of moving pictures. You won't get anywhere playing the ape. You can't be a parrot. 'Experience has taught me,' says Sam Wood, 'that it is safest to drop, as quickly as possible, people who pretend to be what they aren't.'

I asked Paul Boynton, then employment director for a major oil company, what is the biggest mistake people make in applying for jobs. He ought to know: he has interviewed more than sixty thousand job seekers; and he has written a book entitled *6 Ways to Get a Job.* He replied, 'The biggest mistake people make in applying for jobs is in not being themselves. Instead of taking their hair down and being completely frank, they often try to give you the answers they think you want.' But it doesn't work, because nobody wants a phony. Nobody ever wants a counterfeit coin.

A certain daughter of a streetcar conductor had to learn that lesson the hard way. She longed to be a singer. But her face was her misfortune. She had a large mouth and protruding buck teeth. When she first sang in public—in a New Jersey night club—she tried to pull down her upper lip to cover her teeth. She tried to act 'glamorous'. The results? She made herself ridiculous. She was headed for failure.

However, there was a man in this night club who heard the

girl sing and thought she had talent. 'See here,' he said bluntly, 'I've been watching your performance and I know what it is you're trying to hide. You're ashamed of your teeth!' The girl was embarrassed, but the man continued, 'What of it? Is there any particular crime in having buck teeth? Don't try to hide them! Open your mouth, and the audience will love you when they see you're not ashamed. Besides,' he said shrewdly, 'those teeth you're trying to hide may make your fortune!'

Cass Daley took his advice and forgot about her teeth. *From that time on,* she thought only about her audience. She opened her mouth wide and sang with such gusto and enjoyment that she became a top star in movies and radio. Other comedians tried to copy *her!*

The renowned William James was speaking of people who had never found themselves when he declared that the average person develops only ten percent of his or her latent mental abilities. 'Compared to what we ought to be,' he wrote, 'we are only half awake. We are making use of only a small part of our physical and mental resources. Stating the thing broadly, human individuals thus far live within their limits. They possess powers of various sorts which they habitually fail to use.'

YOU'RE THE FIRST OF YOUR KIND

You and I have such abilities, so let's not waste a second worrying because we are not like other people. You are something new in this world. Never before, since the beginning of time, has there ever been anybody exactly like you; and never again throughout all the ages to come will there ever be anybody exactly like you again. The science of genetics informs us that you are what you are largely as a result of twenty-four chromosomes contributed by your father and twenty-four chromosomes contributed by your mother. These forty-eight chromosomes comprise everything that determines what you inherit. 'In each chromosome there may be,' says Amram Scheinfeld, 'anywhere from scores to hundreds of genes—with a single gene, in some cases, able to change the whole life of an individual.' Truly, we are ;fearfully and wonderfully' made.

Even after your mother and father met and mated, there was only one chance in 300,000 billion that the person who is specifically you would be born! In other words, if you had 300,000 billion brothers and sisters, they might all have been different from you. Is all this guesswork? No. It is a scientific fact. If you would like to read more about it, consult *You and Heredity,* by Amram Scheinfeld.

I can talk with conviction about this subject of being yourself because I feel deeply about it. I know what I am talking about. I know from bitter and costly experience. To illustrate: when I first came to New York from the cornfields of Missouri, I enrolled in the American Academy of Dramatic Arts. I aspired to be an actor. I had what I thought was a brilliant idea, a shortcut to success, an idea so simple, so fool proof, that I couldn't understand why thousands of ambitious people hadn't already discovered it. It was this: I would study how the famous actors of that day—John Drew, Walter Hampden, and Otis Skinner—got their effects. Then I would imitate the best points of each one of them and make myself into a shining, triumphant combination of all of them. How silly! How absurd! I had to waste years of my life imitating other people before it penetrated through my thick Missouri skull that I had to be myself and that I couldn't possibly be anyone else.

That distressing experience ought to have taught me a lasting lesson. But it didn't. Not me. I was too dumb. I had to learn it all over again. Several years later, I set out to write what I hoped would be the best book on public speaking for businessmen that had ever been written. I had the same foolish idea about writing this book that I had formerly had about acting: I was going to *borrow* the ideas of a lot of other writers and put them all in one book—a book that would have everything. So I got scores of books on public speaking and spent a year incorporating their ideas into my manuscript. But it finally dawned on me once again that I was playing the fool. This hodgepodge of other men's ideas that I had written was so synthetic, so dull, that no businessman would ever plod through it. So I tossed a year's work into the wastebasket and started all over again. This time I said to myself, 'You've got to be Dale Carnegie, with all his faults and limitations. You can't possibly be anybody else.' So I quit trying to be a combination of other men, and rolled up my sleeves and did what I should have done in the first place: I wrote a textbook on public speaking out of my own experiences, observations, and convictions as a speaker and a teacher of speaking. I learned—for all time, I hope—the lesson that Sir Walter Raleigh learned. (I am *not* talking about the Sir Walter who threw his coat in the mud for the queen to step on. I am talking about the Sir Walter Raleigh who was professor of English literature at Oxford back in 1904.) 'I can't write a book commensurate with Shakespeare,' he said, 'but I can write a book by me.'

Be yourself. Act on the sage advice that Irving Berlin gave the late George Gershwin. When Berlin and Gershwin first met, Berlin was famous but Gershwin was a struggling young composer working for thirty-five dollars a week in Tin Pan Alley. Berlin, impressed by Gershwin's ability, offered Gershwin a job as his musical secretary at almost three times the salary he was then getting. 'But don't take the job,' Berlin advised. 'If you do, you may develop into a second-rate Berlin. But if you insist on being yourself, someday you'll become a first-rate Gershwin.'

Gershwin heeded that warning and slowly transformed himself into one of the significant American composers of his generation.

Charlie Chaplin, Will Rogers, Mary Margaret McBride, Gene Autry, and millions of others had to learn the lesson I am trying to hammer home in this chapter. They had to learn the hard way—just as I did.

When Charlie Chaplin first started making films, the director of the picture insisted on Chaplin's imitating a popular German comedian of that day. Charlie Chaplin got nowhere until he acted himself. Bob Hope had a similar experience: spent years in a singing-and-dancing act—and got nowhere until he began to wisecrack and be himself. Will Rogers twirled a rope in vaudeville for years without saying a word. He got nowhere until he discovered his unique gift for humour and began to talk as he twirled his rope.

When Mary Margaret McBride first went on the air, she tried to be an Irish comedian and failed. When she tried to be just what she was—a plain country girl from Missouri—she became one of the most popular radio stars in New York.

When Gene Autry tried to get rid of his Texas accent and dressed like city boys and claimed he was from New York, people merely laughed behind his back. But when he started twanging his banjo and singing cowboy ballads, Gene Autry started out on a career that made him the world's most popular cowboy both in pictures and on the radio.

You are something new in this world. Be glad of it. Make the most of what nature gave you. In the last analysis, all art is autobiographical. You can sing only what you are. You can paint only what you are. You must be what your experiences, your environment, and your heredity have made you. For better or for worse, you must cultivate your own little garden. For better or for worse, you must play your own little instrument in the orchestra of life.

As Emerson said in his essay on 'Self-Reliance': 'There is a time in every man's education when he arrives at the conviction that envy is ignorance; that imitation is suicide; that he must take himself for better, for worse, as his portion; that though the wide universe is full of good, no kernel of nourishing corn can come to him but through his toil bestowed on that plot of ground which is given to him to till. The power which resides in him is new in nature, and none but he knows what that is which he can do, nor does he know until he has tried.'

POINTS TO REMEMBER

1. No matter what happens, always be yourself!
2. Stop imitating others.
3. Let's not waste a second worrying because you are not like other people. You are something new in this world.